STANDARD TUNING EDITION

Teach Yourself To Play Ukulele

MORTY MANUS & RON MANUS

Everything you need to know to start playing now!

- Teaches you how to play the ukulele with an easy-to-follow approach that makes learning fun
- Different strumming techniques help you play in any style
- Includes great folk, blues and country songs with lyrics
- Teaches you how to play by ear

Inspired by and dedicated to Ken Moore.

Alfred Music
Van Nuys, CA 91410-0003
alfred.com

ISBN-10: 0-7390-6340-5 Book
ISBN-13: 978-0-7390-6340-8 Book

ISBN-10: 0-7390-7753-8 Book & CD
ISBN-13: 978-0-7390-7753-5 Book & CD

ISBN-10: 0-7390-7351-6 DVD
ISBN-13: 978-0-7390-7351-3 DVD

ISBN-10: 0-7390-7402-4 Book, CD & DVD (DVD in case)
ISBN-13: 978-0-7390-7402-2 Book, CD & DVD (DVD in case)

ISBN-10: 0-7390-7403-2 Book, CD & DVD (DVD bound in)
ISBN-13: 978-0-7390-7403-9 Book, CD & DVD (DVD bound in)

Cover photograph courtesy of the Martin Guitar Company.

CONTENTS

FOREWORD

Since the time of World War I the ukulele has been one of the most popular instruments of musical hobbyists in America. Its ease of playing, portability and reasonable price put it within reach of many players who otherwise would wind up listening to others rather than entertaining themselves and their friends. Although the uke is not as popular today as it was in its heyday, the Jazz Age, it is still the instrument of choice for those who love to sing and play.

This book is designed to teach you the basic skills of playing this fun instrument. Just about everything you need to know is between these covers, including how to tune, how to strum and how to play all the basic chords. Plus, this book gives you words and music to folk songs, blues songs, country songs and popular tunes so you can have fun while learning techniques and chords which will allow you to play and sing virtually any song you wish. We've even included a section on how to play by ear, a section on how to transpose (take a song written in one key and play it in a different key), plus chord diagrams in every key in the most commonly used tuning.

We commend you on your choice of this fun, easy-to-play instrument and suggest that you not waste a minute getting started. You'll be playing songs and having fun before you know it!

A SHORT HISTORY OF THE UKULELE

In 1879 three instrument makers emigrated from Madeira, near Portugal, to Hawaii. They brought with them a small guitar-like instrument called a *machête da braça*. By the turn of the century, it had been enthusiastically adopted by the native Hawaiians and renamed, perhaps because of the motion of the pick above the strings, ukulele, or "jumping flea." In the early 1900s, the ukulele was discovered by American college students and by 1916 it had become a fad.

The uke, as it was familiarly called, was cheap to buy, easy to carry and simple to play. It was perfectly suited for accompanying pop tunes of the day like "Ain't She Sweet" and "Five Foot Two, Eyes of Blue," as well as traditional folk songs, cowboy songs, and even blues and ragtime. All during Prohibition (1920–1933) the uke was a favorite at parties both on and off the campus. During the 1930s the uke was gradually replaced by the guitar which, although more difficult to play, was better suited to the tastes of the day. Then in the late '40s and '50s the ukulele became popular again, largely because it was featured by Arthur Godfrey on his hugely successful show, "Arthur Godfrey's Talent Scouts."

But the uke has always been popular. Much of the sheet music published from 1920 to 1950 included ukulele chord diagrams. It's only since the advent of rock in the '50s that these have been replaced with guitar chord diagrams. Today, the ukulele is still one of the most popular instruments of musical hobbyists. Even if you've had no musical training, in a short time you'll be able to master enough chords to accompany hundreds of pop songs, folk songs, country songs and blues songs and will soon be able to enjoy playing and singing with your ukulele.

(Note: "Ukulele" is the preferred spelling, but "ukelele" is not incorrect.)

GETTING STARTED

THE UKULELE

The ukulele is strummed with the right hand. Depending on what kind of sound is desired, you can use a felt pick, the right thumb, or the fingernail of your index finger. The strings are strummed with a downward motion in the approximate area of the 10th fret. Later we'll show you other ways of strumming the uke.

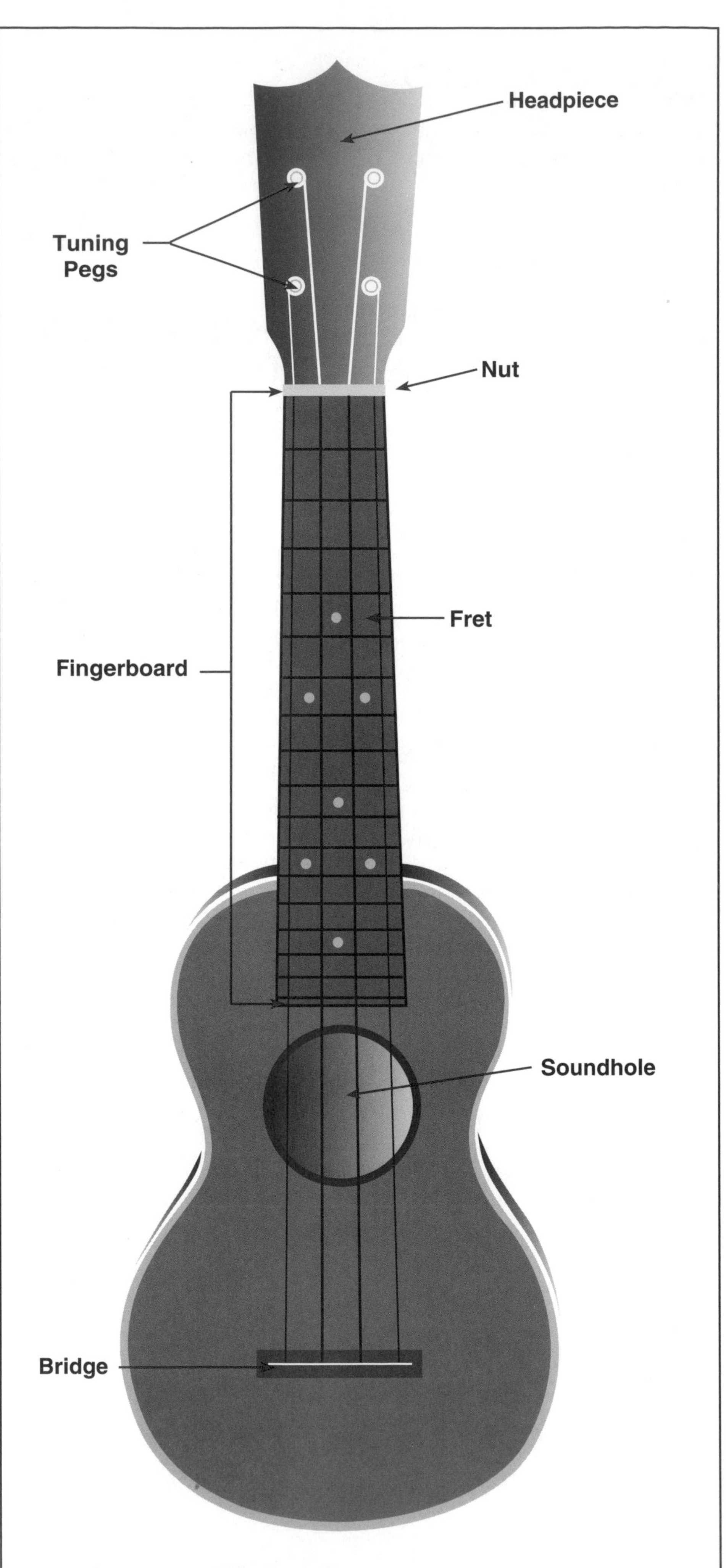

HOW TO HOLD THE UKULELE

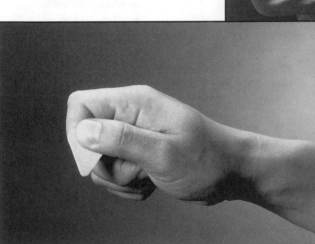

▲ *How to hold the felt pick.*

When playing, keep your left wrist away from the fingerboard. This allows your fingers to be in a better position to finger the chords.

Press your fingers firmly, directly behind the fret but not on them. Make sure your fingers do not touch any neighboring strings.

HOW TO TUNE YOUR UKULELE

Tune the four strings of your ukulele to the same pitch as the four notes shown on the piano in the following illustration:

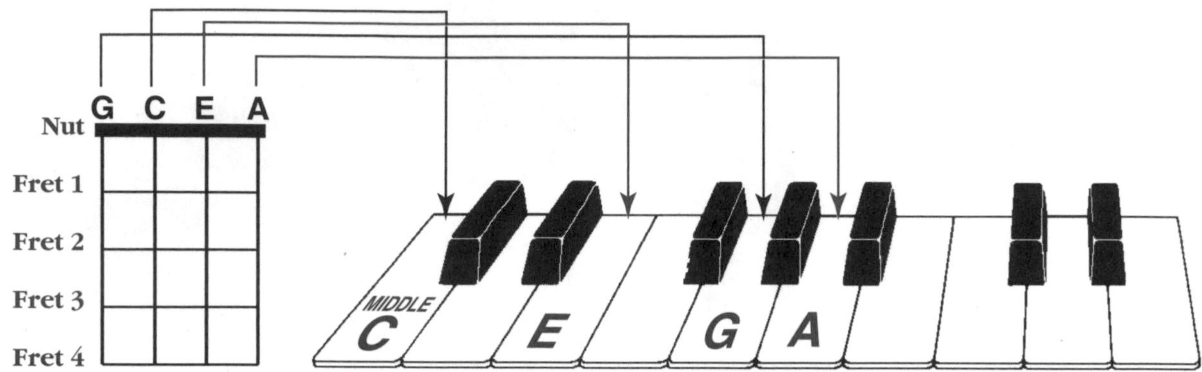

Other Ways of Tuning Your Ukulele

Tune the 1st string to A on the piano. If no piano is available, approximate A as best you can and proceed as follows:

Press fret 5 of string 2 and tune it to the pitch of string 1 (A)

Press fret 4 of string 3 and tune it to the pitch of string 2 (E)

Press fret 2 of string 4 and tune it to the pitch of string 1 (A)

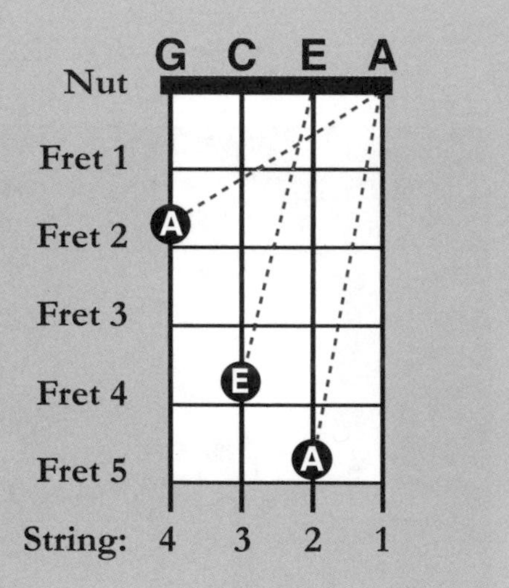

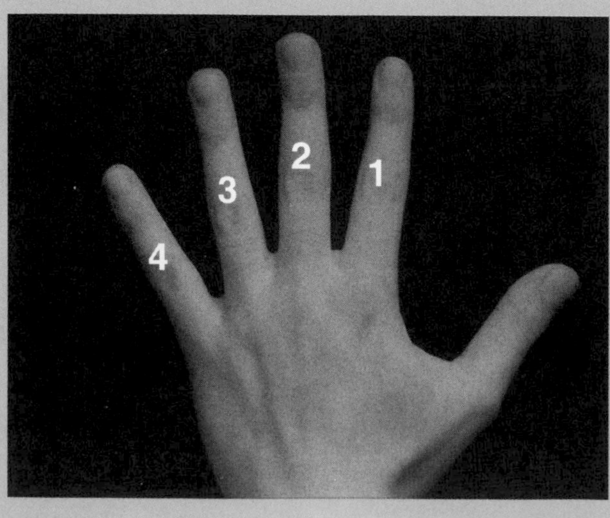

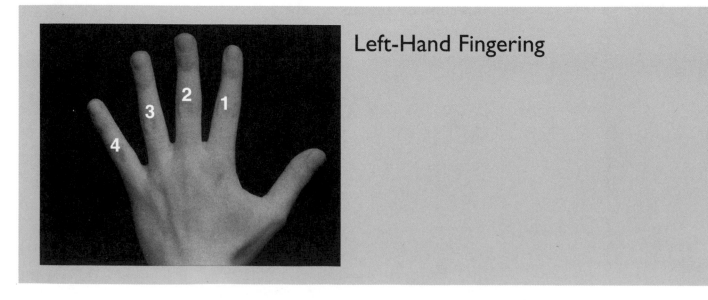

Left-Hand Fingering

GETTING STARTED

GETTING ACQUAINTED WITH MUSIC

Notes

Musical sounds are indicated by symbols called NOTES. Their time value is determined by their color (white or black) and by stems and flags attached to the note.

The Staff

The name and pitch of the notes are determined by the note's position on five horizontal lines and the spaces in between, called the STAFF. The notes are named after the first seven letters of the alphabet (A–G), repeated to embrace the entire range of musical sound.

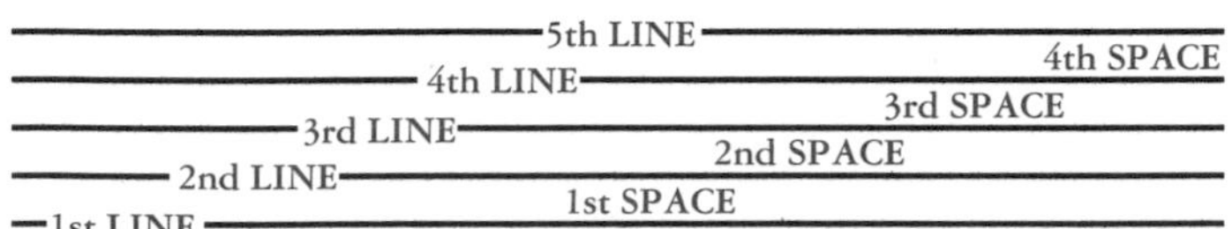

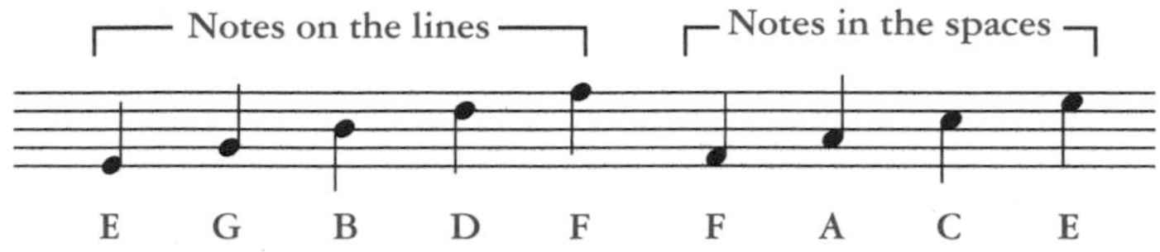

Measures and Bar Lines

Music is also divided into equal parts, called MEASURES. One measure is divided from another by a BAR LINE.

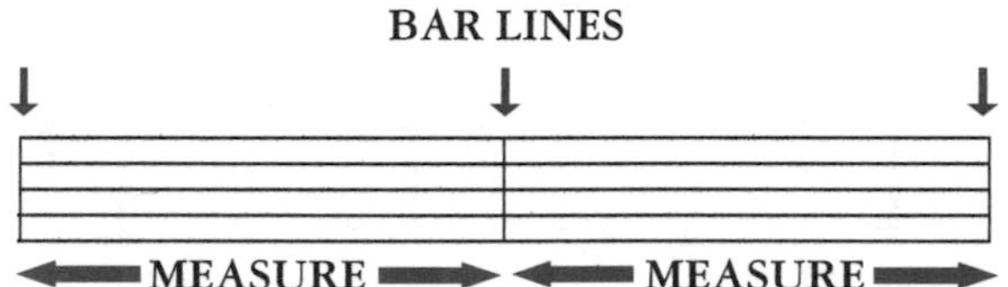

Clefs

During the evolution of music notation, the staff had from two to twenty lines, and symbols were invented to locate a reference line, or pitch, by which all other pitches were determined. These symbols were called CLEFS.

Music for the uke is written in the G or treble clef. Originally the Gothic letter G was used on a four-line staff to establish the pitch of G:

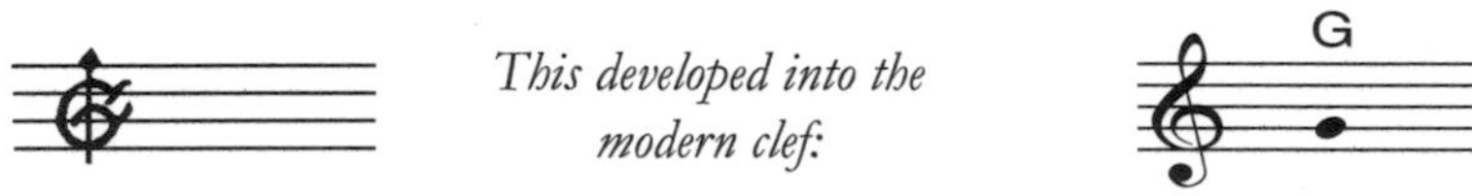

Flats ♭, Sharps ♯ and Naturals ♮

A FLAT SIGN ♭ lowers the pitch of a note a half step.

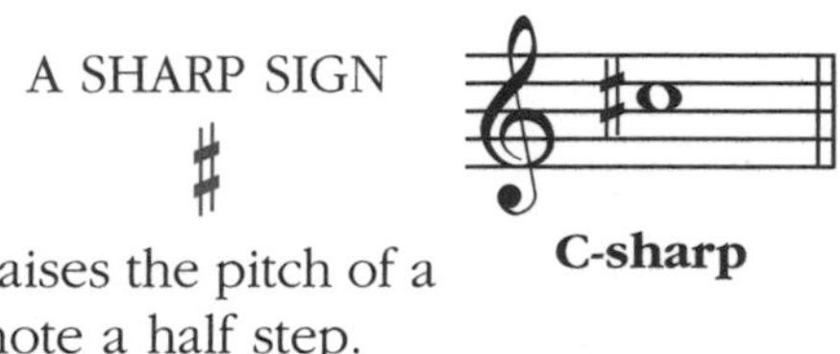

A SHARP SIGN ♯ raises the pitch of a note a half step.

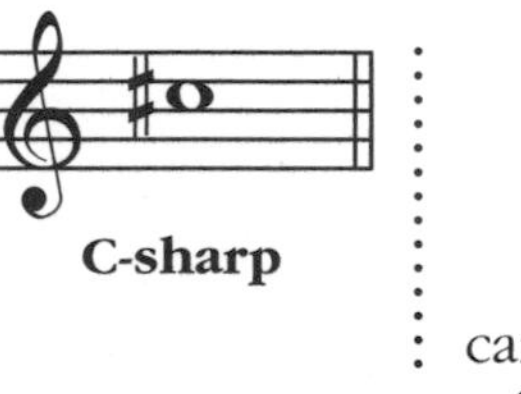

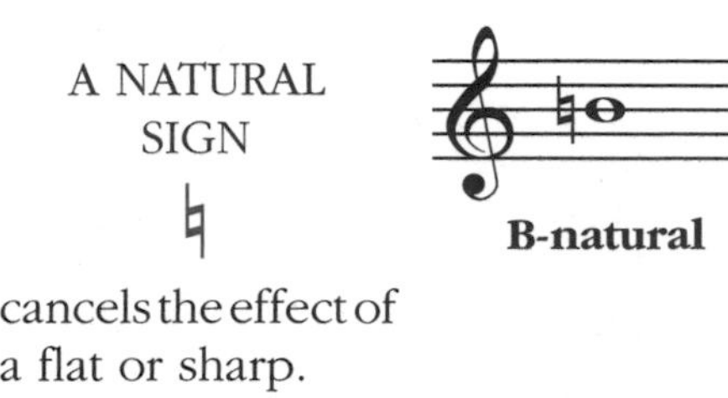

A NATURAL SIGN ♮ cancels the effect of a flat or sharp.

Key Signatures

To make the writing process easier, we can indicate the flats or sharps to be used in a composition at the beginning of the piece. This is called a KEY SIGNATURE and tells the performer that the accidentals (flats and sharps) indicated are in effect throughout the piece.

For example the F♯ in this key signature, which appears on the top line of the staff immediately following the clef, indicates that all of the F's in this composition are to be played F♯.

Key Signature of G Major

How to Play the C7 Chord

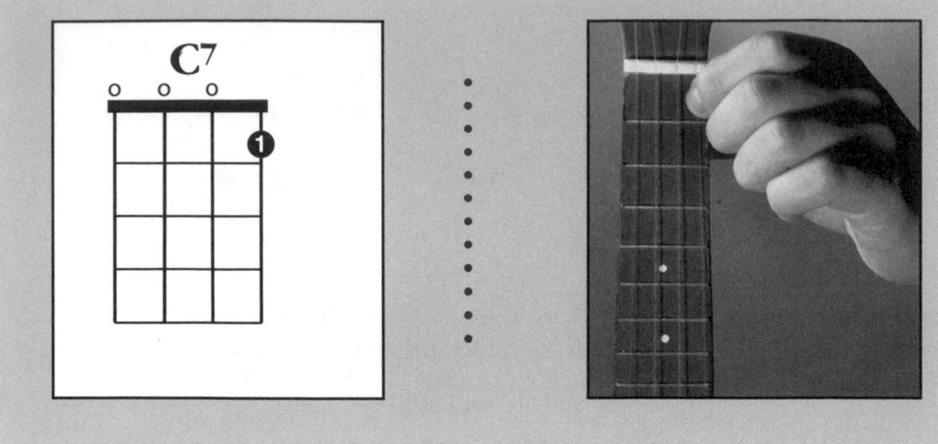

o means open string (string is not fingered)

- - - - - - - - - - - - - line means string is not played

Place ❶ in position, then play one string at a time:

Play all four strings together:

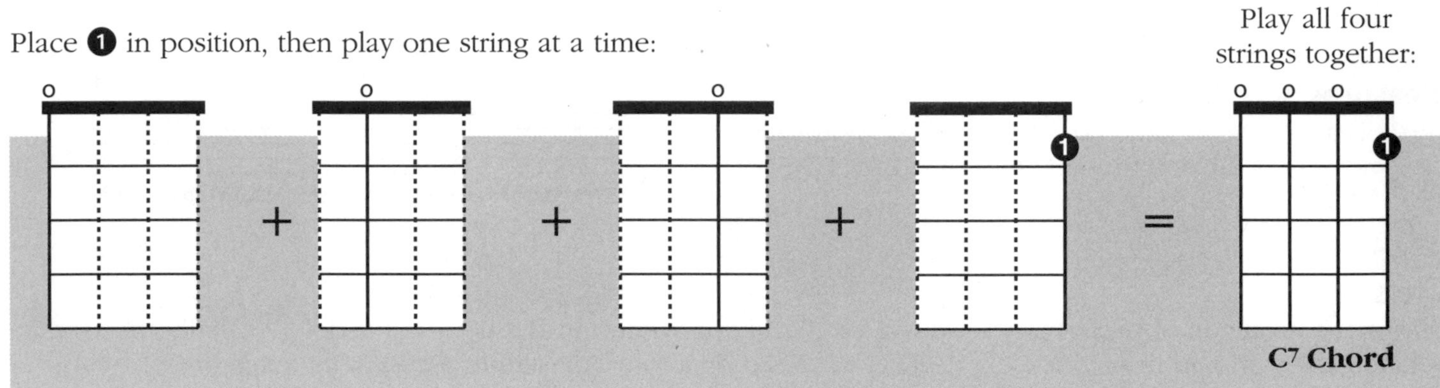

Play slowly and evenly. Each / (slash mark) means to repeat the previous chord. Strum downward for each chord name and slash mark. Use your thumb or a felt pick. The chord name is repeated in each measure.

Play slowly and evenly:

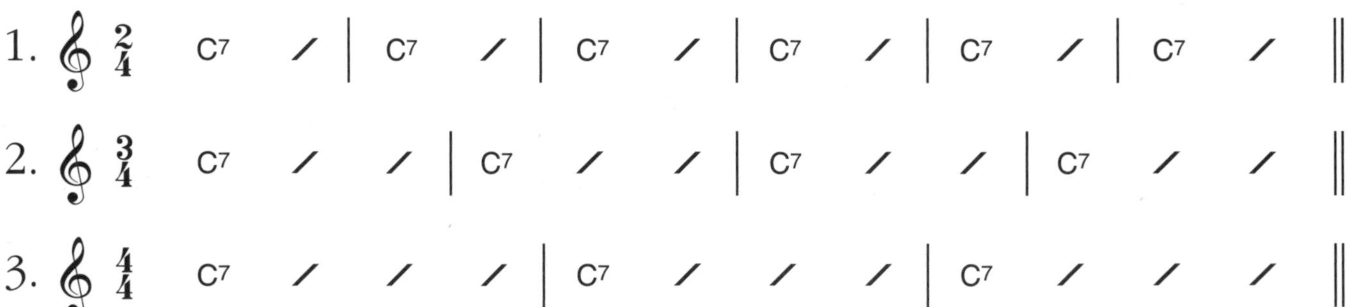

MINI MUSIC LESSON

TIME SIGNATURES

At the beginning of every piece of music, immediately after the clef, there's a fraction such as 2/4, 3/4 or 4/4, called a time signature. The upper number indicates how many beats are in each measure. For example, in 4/4, we know there will be four beats in each measure. The lower number indicates what type of note gets one beat. For example, when the lower number is a 4, we know that each quarter note (see Note Values on page 9) gets one beat. If the lower number is 8, an eighth note gets one beat.

How to Play the F Chord

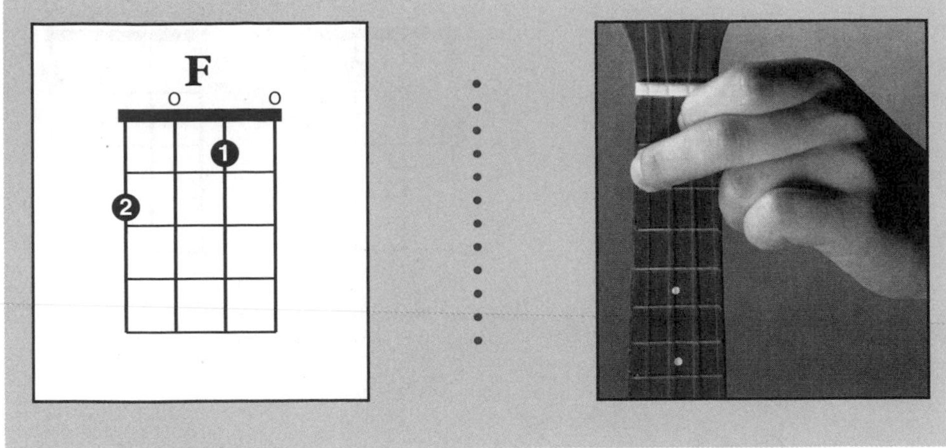

Place ❶ and ❷ in position, then play one string at a time:

Play all four strings together:

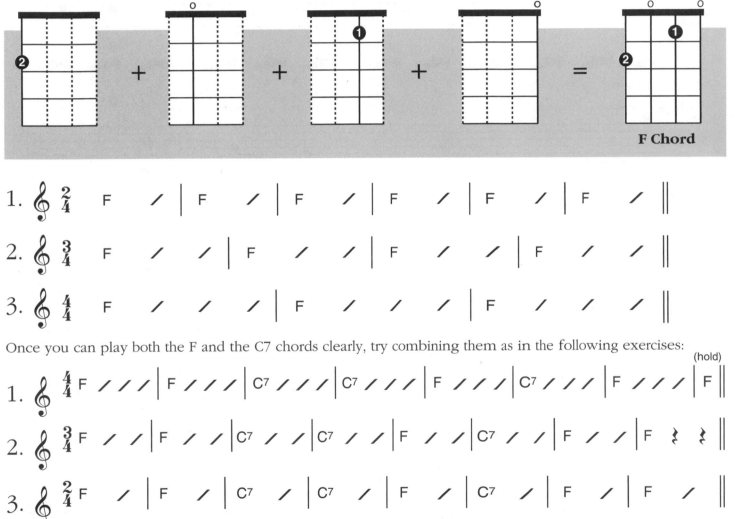

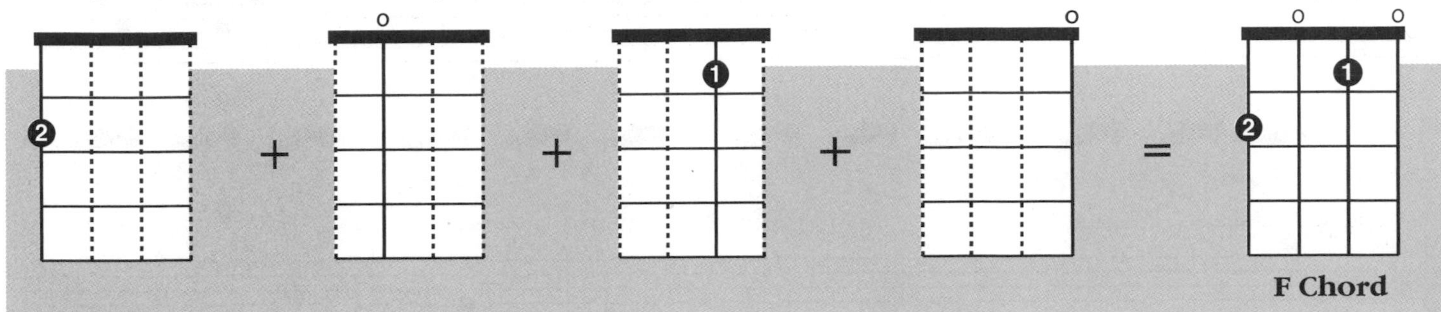

1. 2/4 F / | F / | F / | F / | F / | F / ||

2. 3/4 F / / | F / / | F / / | F / / ||

3. 4/4 F / / / | F / / / | F / / / ||

Once you can play both the F and the C7 chords clearly, try combining them as in the following exercises:

1. 4/4 F / / / | F / / / | C7 / / / | C7 / / / | F / / / | C7 / / / | F / / / | F (hold) ||

2. 3/4 F / / | F / / | C7 / / | C7 / / | F / / | C7 / / | F / / | F 𝄽 𝄽 ||

3. 2/4 F / | F / | C7 / | C7 / | F / | C7 / | F / | F / ||

NOTE VALUES

The shape of the note tells you how long to play it.

- ♩ = Quarter note (1 beat)
- 𝅗𝅥 = Half note (2 beats)
- 𝅗𝅥. = Dotted half note (3 beats)
- 𝅝 = Whole note (4 beats)

REST VALUES

Rests are measured silences used in music. For each note, there is a corresponding rest.

- 𝄽 = Quarter rest (silence for 1 beat)
- 𝄼 = Half rest (silence for 2 beats)
- 𝄼. = Dotted half rest (silence for 3 beats)
- 𝄻 = Whole rest (silence for 4 beats)

MINI MUSIC LESSON

TIES

This curved line is called a tie. It connects two or more notes and ties them together. Play or sing the note once and hold it for the value of both (or more) tied notes.

The chords used in this song are:

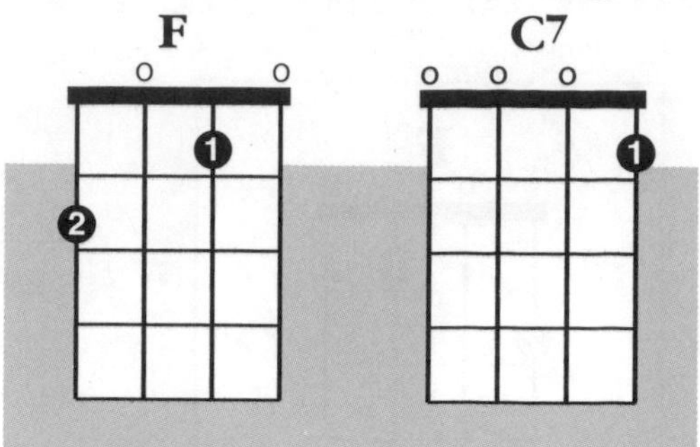

Down in the Valley

American Folk Song

To hear the first note of the song, look up fingering on page 57. In this case, play the note C.

Key Signature: remember to play all B's a ½ step lower, B♭.

Moderately

F / / F / / F / / F / /
Down in the val - ley, val - ley so

Count: 1 2 3 1 2 3 1 2 3 1 2 3
Tap:

C7 / / C7 / / C7 / / C7 / /
low,_____ Hang your head o -

Tie

C7 / / C7 / / F / / F / /
ver, hear the wind blow,_____

Tie

F / / F / / F / / F / /
Hear the wind blow, boys, hear the wind

C7 / / C7 / / C7 / / C7 / /
blow,_____ Hang your head o -

Tie

C7 / / C7 / / F / / F / / F
ver, hear the wind blow._____

Tie

1 (2) Rest (3) Rest

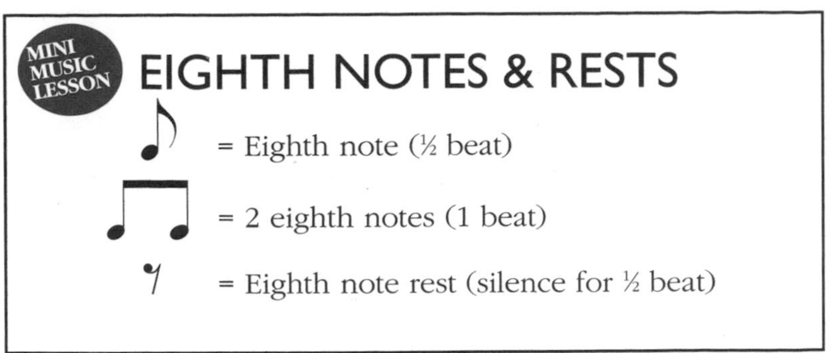

The chords used in this song are:

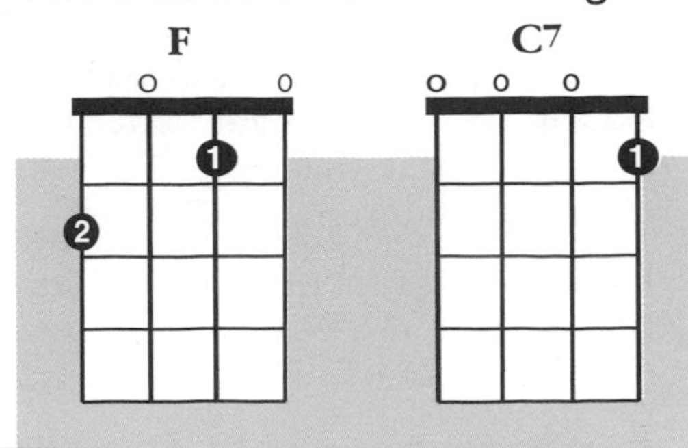

Go Tell Aunt Rhody

American Folk Song

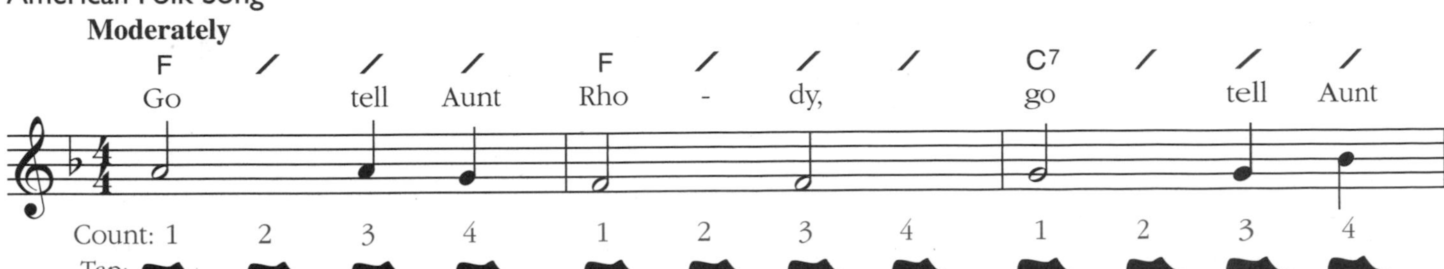

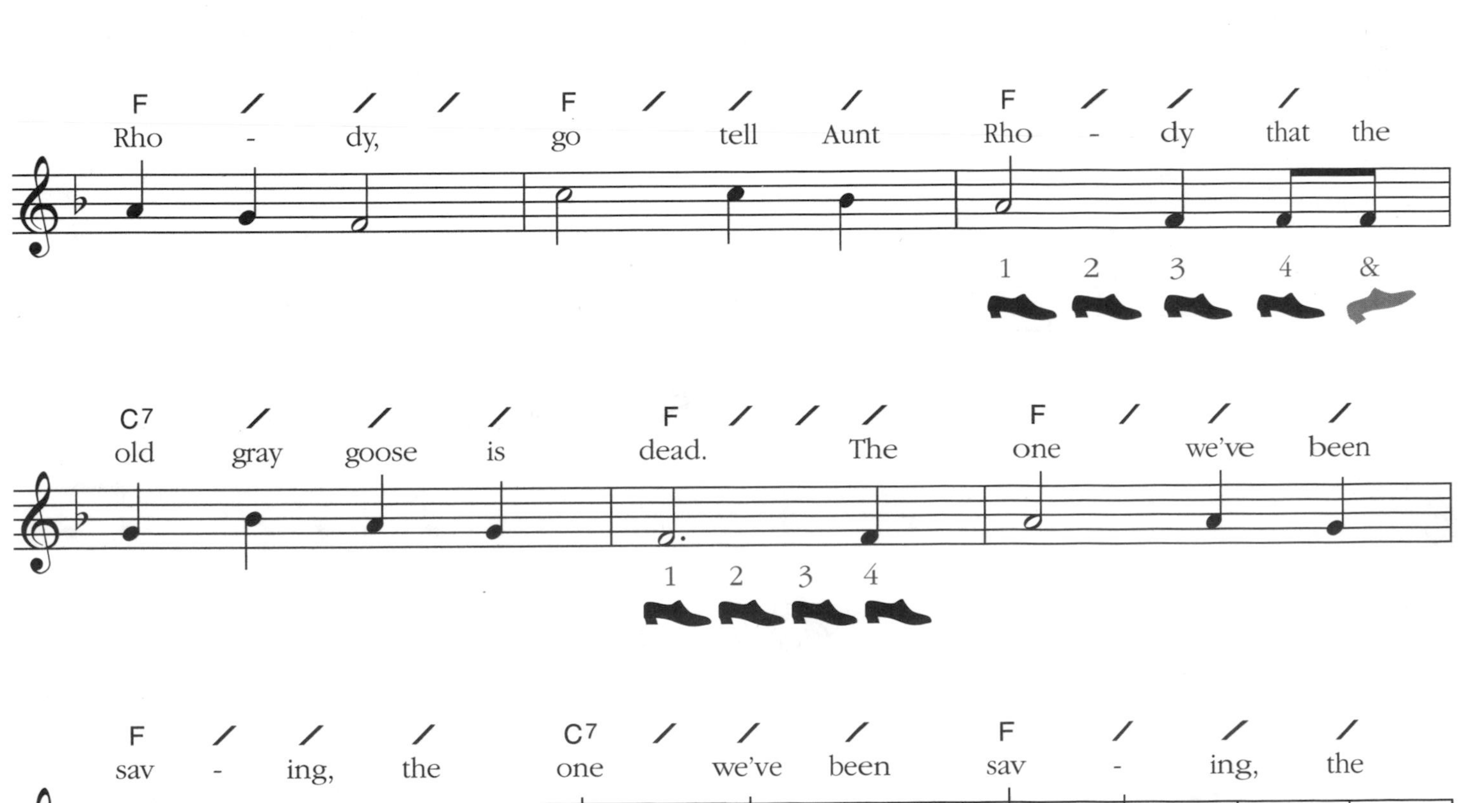

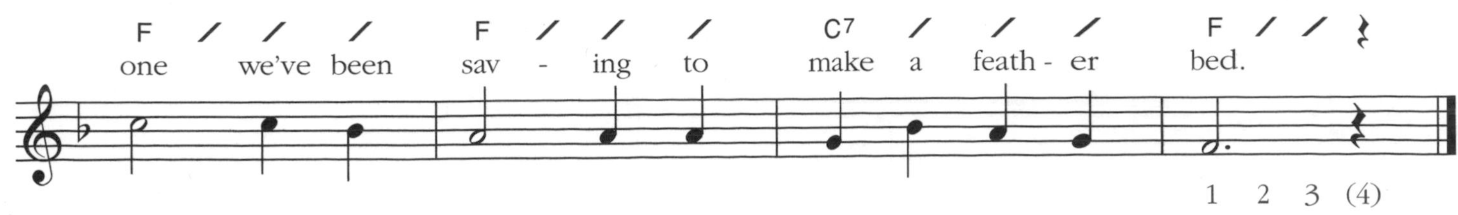

MINI MUSIC LESSON

PICKUP MEASURES

Sometimes a song begins with an incomplete measure called a pickup. The pickup measure contains fewer beats than are called for in the time signature. For example, a 3/4 measure may contain one or two beats. Often (but not always) the last measure of the piece will be missing the same number of beats that the pickup uses. In this way the initial incomplete measure is completed.

Look at the last measure of Cockles and Mussels. It has only two beats. These two beats, plus the one beat in the pickup measure (the first measure), complete one measure of 3/4 time.

DOTTED QUARTER NOTE

A dotted quarter note equals 1½ beats.

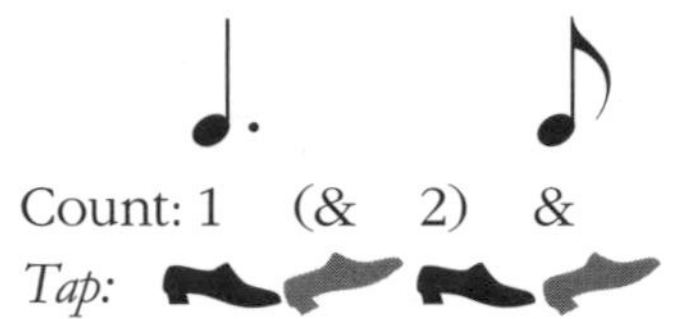

The chords used in this song are:

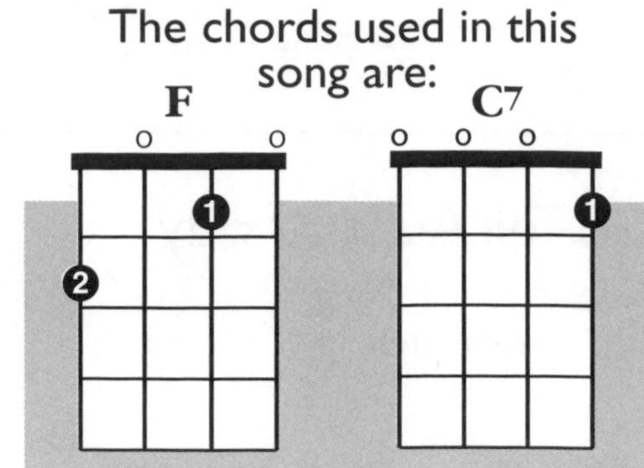

Cockles and Mussels

Irish Folk Melody

Moderately

Pickup Measure

F F C7 C7
In Dub - lin's fair cit - y, where girls are so pret- ty, I

Dotted Quarter Note

Count: 3 1 2 & 3 & 1 & 2 & 3 &

F F C7 C7
first set my eyes on sweet Mol - ly Ma - lone, As she

1 2 & 3 &

F F C7 C7
wheeled her wheel - bar - row through streets broad and nar- row, Cry - ing

1 & 2 & 3 &

F F C7 F C7 F
Cock - les and Mus - sels! a - live, a - live oh!

1 2

Chorus

F F C7 C7
A - live, a - live oh! A - live, a - live oh! Cry - ing

3 Pickup Measure

F C7 F C7 F C7 F
Cock - les and Mus - sels! a - live, a - live oh!

1 2

The chords used in this song are:

F
C7
2
1
1

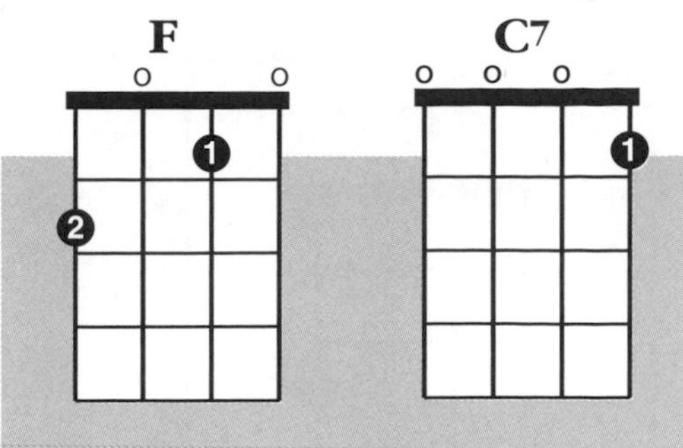

Clementine

American Folk Song

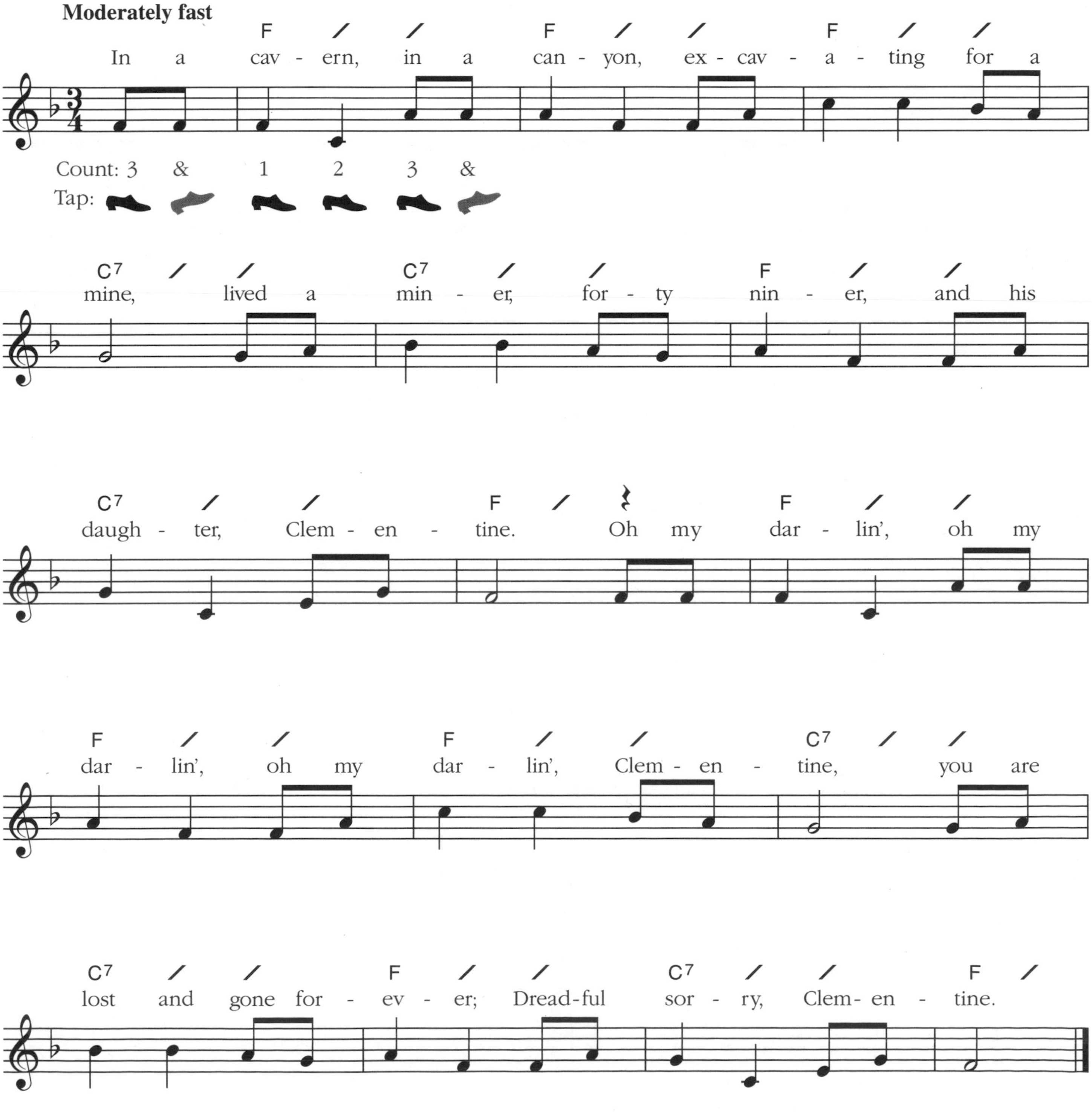

Moderately fast
F / / F / / F / /
In a cav - ern, in a can - yon, ex - cav - a - ting for a
Count: 3 & 1 2 3 &
Tap:
C7 / / C7 / / F / /
mine, lived a min - er, for - ty nin - er, and his
C7 / / F /
daugh - ter, Clem - en - tine. Oh my dar - lin', oh my
F / / F / / C7 / /
dar - lin', oh my dar - lin', Clem - en - tine, you are
C7 / / F / / C7 / / F /
lost and gone for - ev - er; Dread-ful sor - ry, Clem- en - tine.

How to Play the C Chord

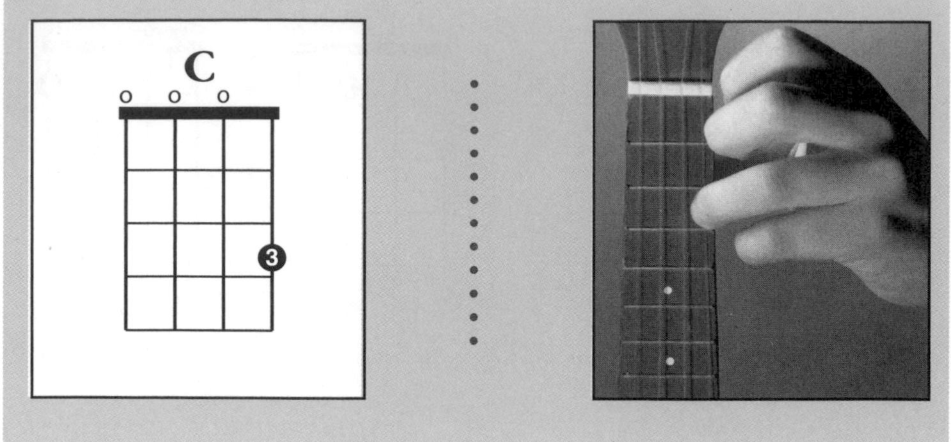

Place ❸ in position, then play one string at a time:

Play all four strings together:

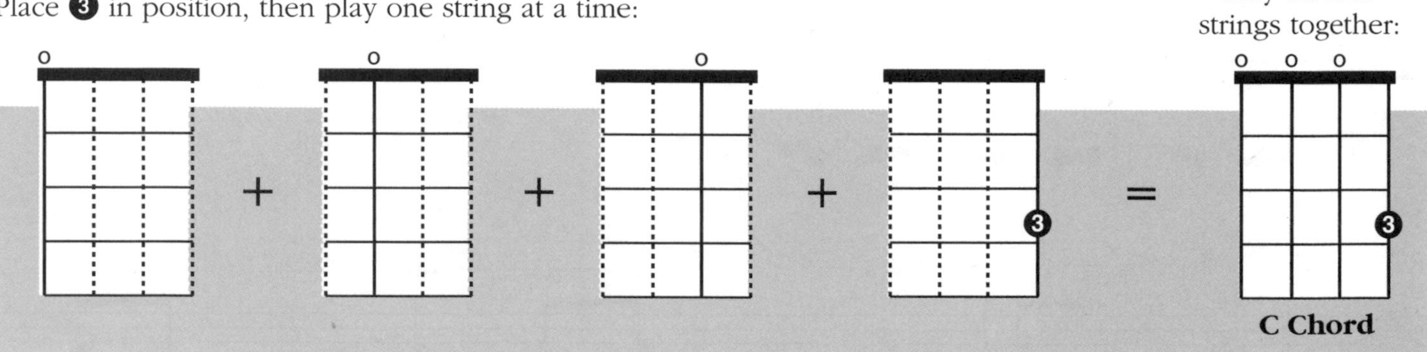

Play slowly and evenly:

1. 2/4 C / | C / | C / | C / | C / | C / ||
2. 3/4 C / / | C / / | C / / | C / / ||
3. 4/4 C / / / | C / / / | C / / / ||

Now try these exercises. They combine all the chords you know:

1. 2/4 C / | C / | C7 / | C7 / | F / | F / | C / | C / ||
2. 3/4 F / / | C / / | F / / | C7 / / | F / / | F 𝄽 𝄽 ||
3. 4/4 C / / / | C7 / / / | F / / / | C / / / | F / / / | C / / / | C / / / ||

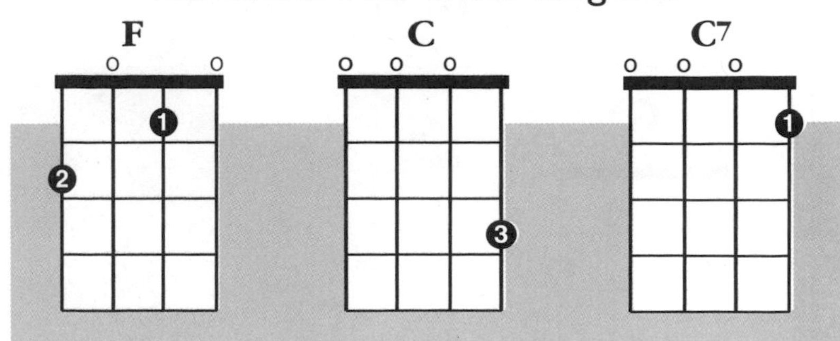

Tom Dooley

American Folk Song

Words and music collected, adapted and arranged by Frank Warner, John A. Lomax and Alan Lomax.

From the singing of Frank Proffitt.

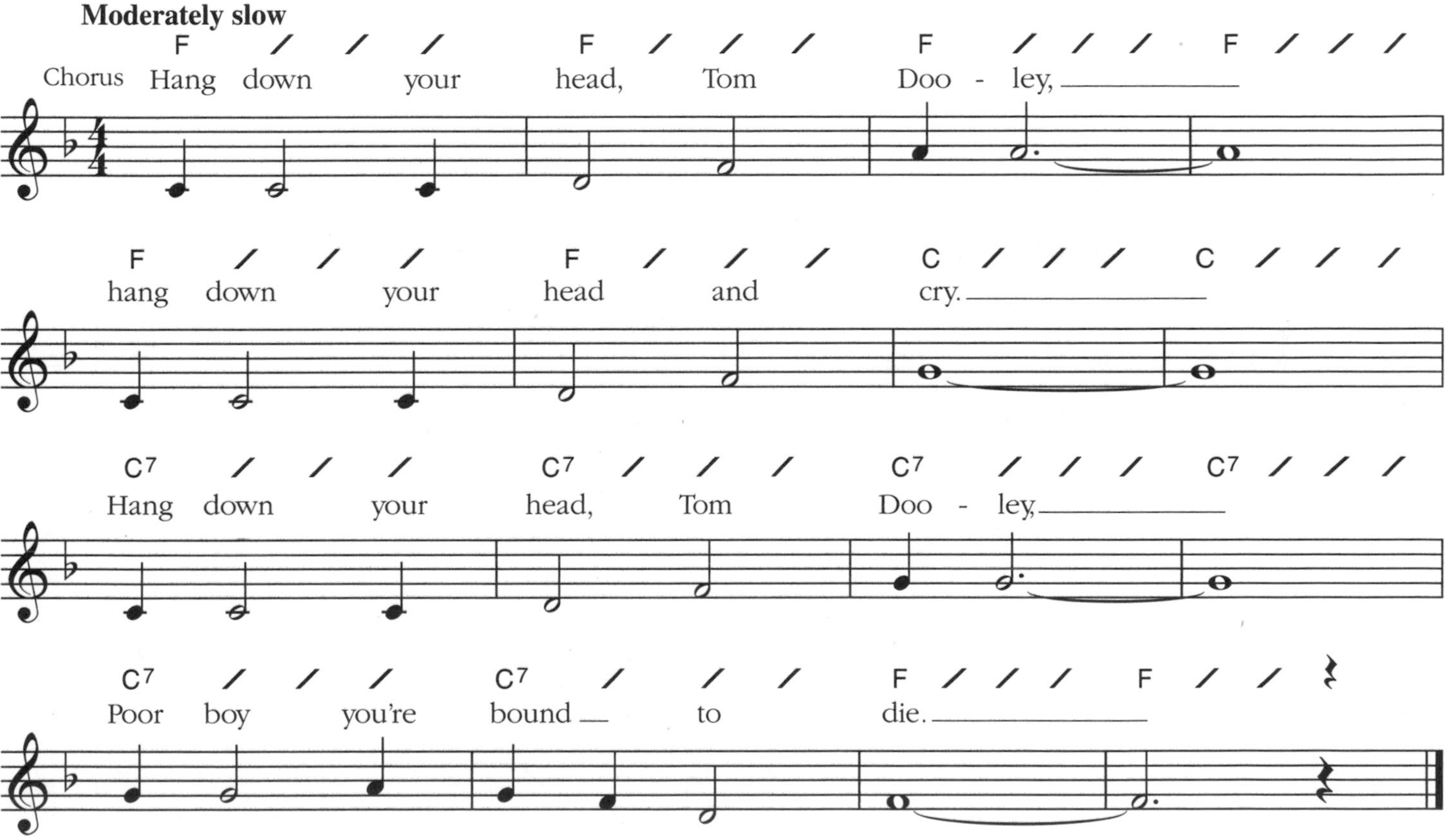

Additional Verses

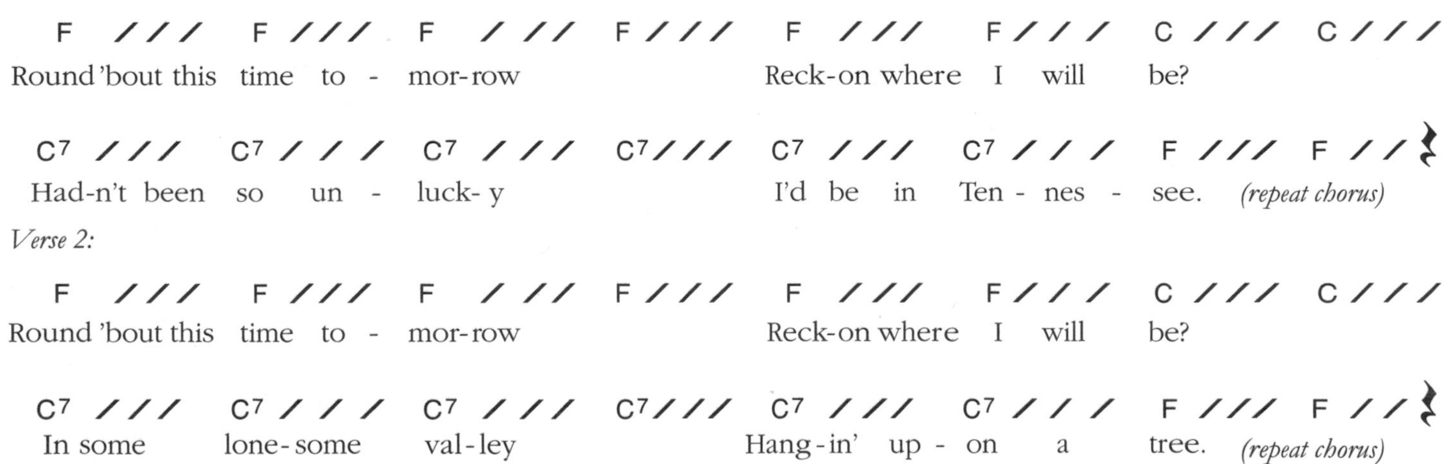

How to Play the G^{7} Chord

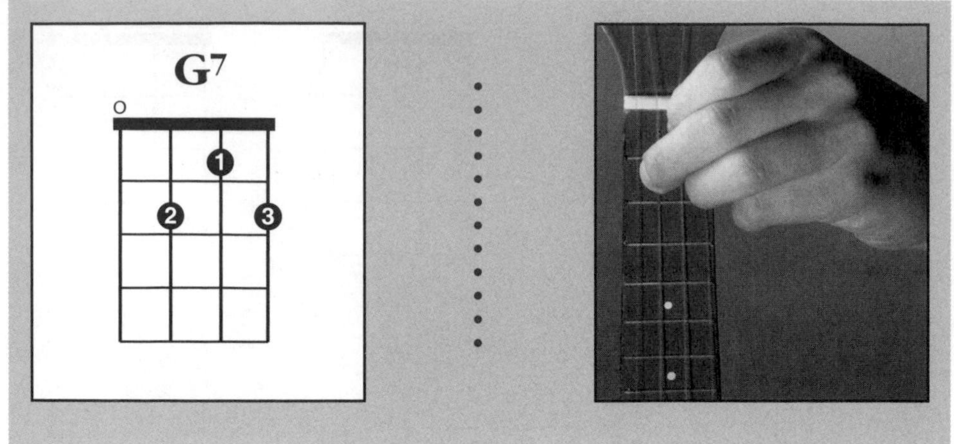

Place ❶, ❷ and ❸ in position, then play one string at a time:

Play all four strings together:

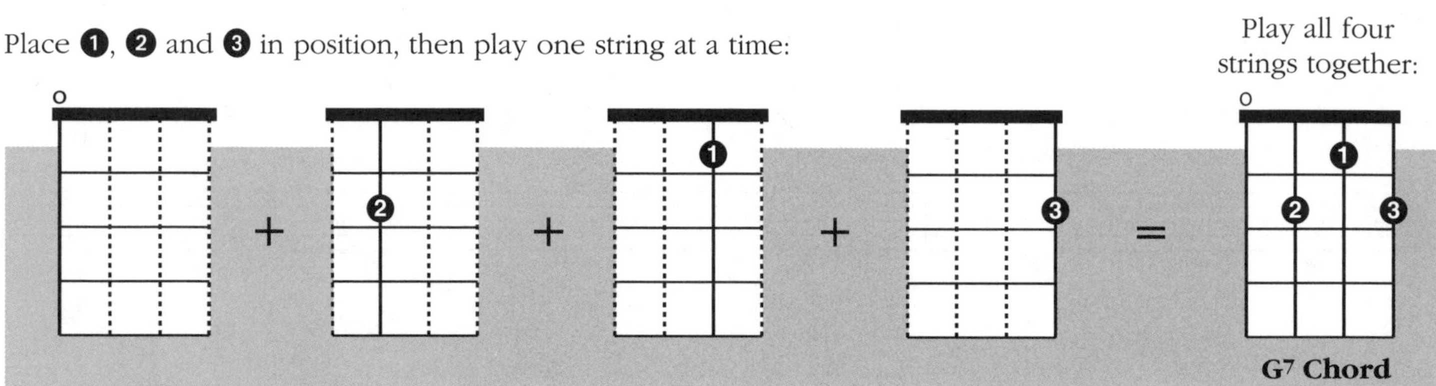

Play slowly and evenly:

1. 4/4 G7 / / / | C / / / | G7 / / / | C / / / ||

2. 3/4 C / / | G7 / / | C / / | G7 / / | C / / | C 𝄽 𝄽 ||

3. 2/4 G7 / | C / | G7 / | C / | F / | C / | G7 / | C / ||

4. 4/4 C / / / | F / / / | C / / / | G7 / / / | C / / / | C / / 𝄽 ||

5. 3/4 C / / | C7 / / | F / / | C / / | F / / | F / / | C / / | C / / |
G7 / / | G7 / / | C / / | F / / | C / / | C 𝄽 𝄽 ||

The chords used in this song are:

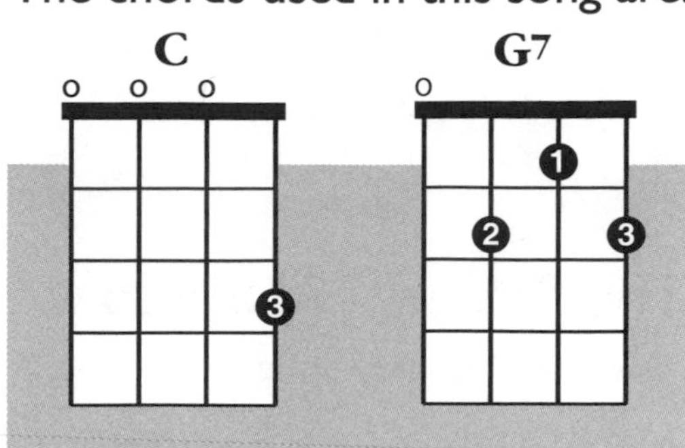

Love Somebody

American Folk Song

Moderately

C / / / G7 / / / C / / / G7 / / /
Love some-bod - y, yes I do; Love some-bod - y, yes I do;

C / / / G7 / / / C / G7 / C / / /
Love some-bod - y, yes I do; Love some-bod- y, but I won't tell who.

C / / / C / / / C / / / G7 / / /
Love some-bod - y, yes I do; Love some-bod - y, yes I do;

C / / / C / / / C / G7 / C / / /
Love some-bod - y, yes I do; And I hope some-bod - y loves me too.

Additional Verses

Verse 2:

C / / / G7 / / /
Love some-bod - y, 'deed I do;

C / / / G7 / / /
Love some-bod - y, now guess who?

C / / / G7 / / /
Love some-bod - y, have you guessed?

C / G7 / C / / /
Love some-bod- y but I won't tell who.

C / / / G7 / / /
Love some-bod - y, yes I do,

(Repeat chorus)

Verse 3:

C / G7 / C / / /
Love some-bod- y but I won't tell who.

C / / / G7 / / /
Love some-bod - y, yes I do,

C / / / G7 / / /
Love some-bod - y, now guess who?

C / / / G7 / / /
Love some-bod - y, have you guessed?

C / G7 / C / /
Some-one 'tween six-teen and twent-y two.

(Repeat chorus)

The chords used in this song are:

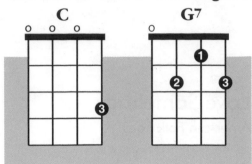

C G7

The Streets of Laredo

American Cowboy Song

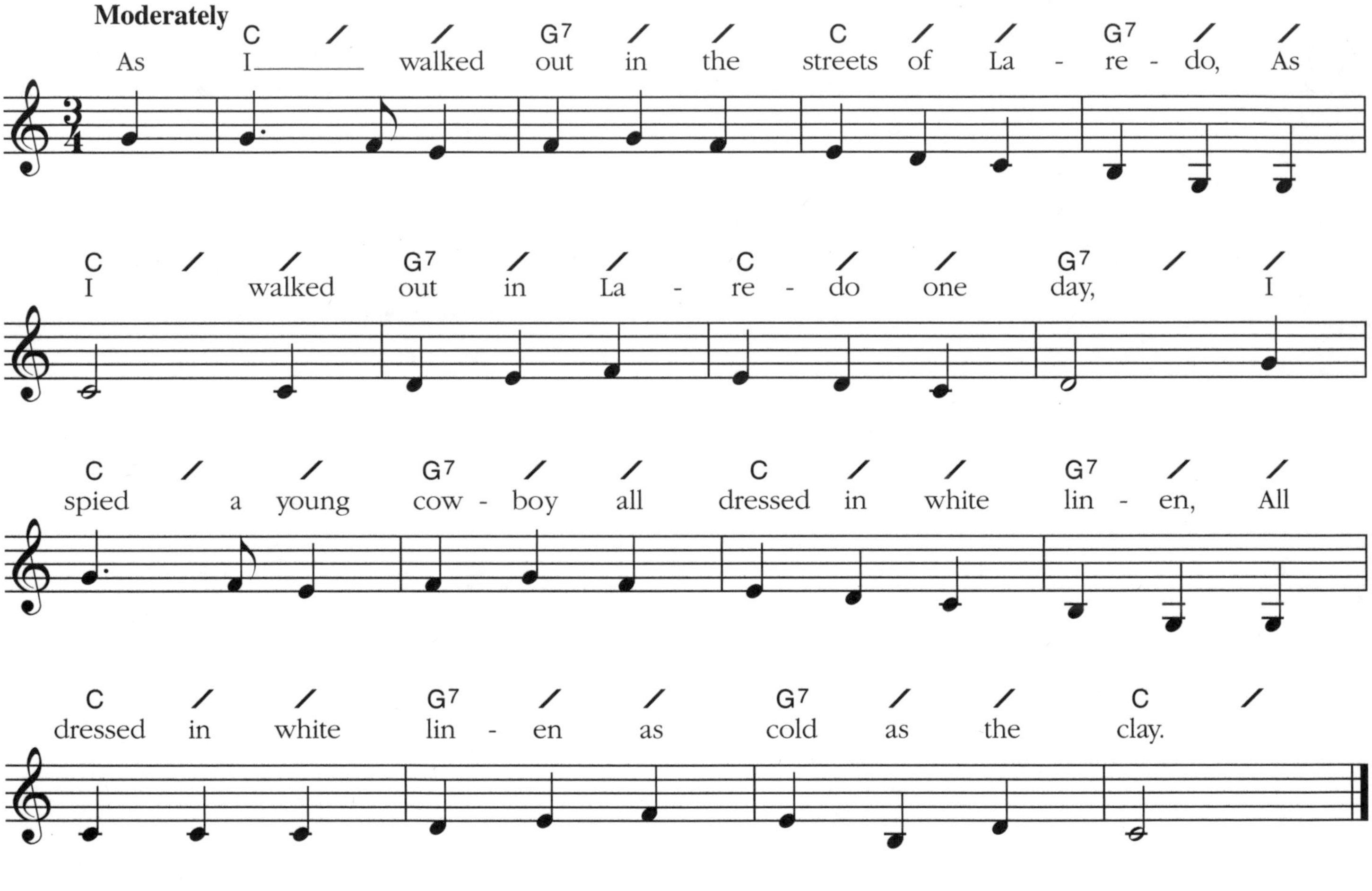

Moderately

C / / G7 / / C / / G7 / /
As I______ walked out in the streets of La - re - do, As

C / / G7 / / C / / G7 / /
I walked out in La - re - do one day, I

C / / G7 / / C / / G7 / /
spied a young cow - boy all dressed in white lin - en, All

C / / G7 / / G7 / / C /
dressed in white lin - en as cold as the clay.

THE DOWN- and UP-STROKE

MINI MUSIC LESSON

You can make your accompaniment of waltz songs like "The Streets of Laredo" more interesting by replacing the second beat of the measure with a down-stroke followed by an up-stroke. The symbol for down-stroke is ⊓; an up-stroke is called for by the sign V. Together, the down- and up-stroke take as much time as a regular strum.

Try the following exercise. When you can do it smoothly, use it to accompany this song.

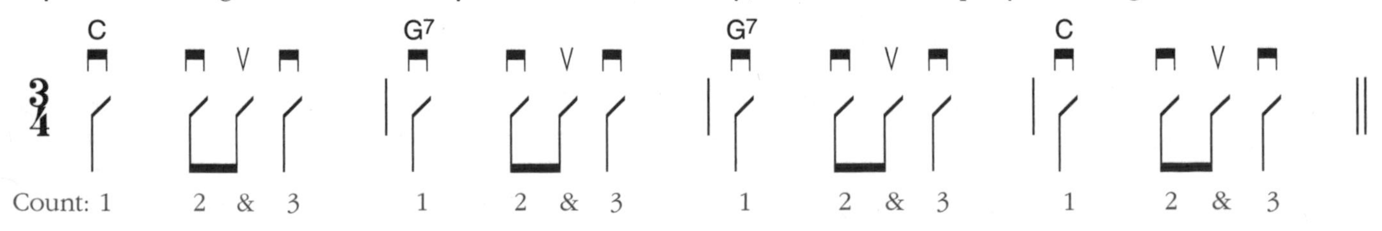

The chords used in this song are:

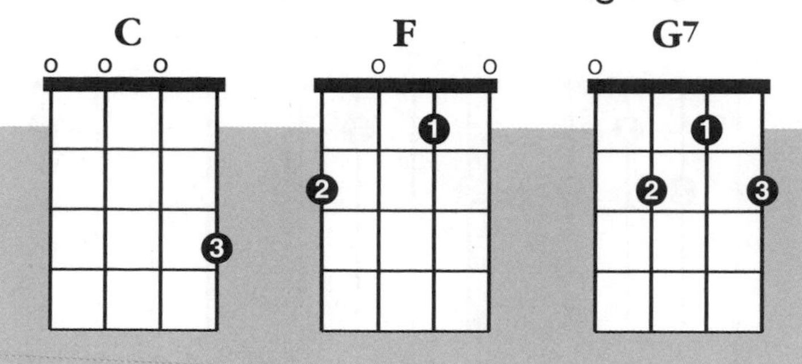

THE FERMATA 𝄐

The sign 𝄐 is called a fermata.
It means to hold the note it is over a little longer.

Michael, Row the Boat Ashore

Folk Song from the Sea Islands of Georgia

Additional Verses

Verse 2:

(C ⁄) C ⁄ ⁄ ⁄ C ⁄ ⁄ ⁄ F ⁄ ⁄ ⁄ C ⁄
Sis - ter help to trim the sail, hal - le - lu - jah!

(C ⁄) C ⁄ ⁄ ⁄ G7 ⁄ ⁄ ⁄ C ⁄ G7 ⁄ C 𝄐
Sis - ter, help to trim the sail, hal - le - lu - jah!

Verse 3:

(C ⁄) C ⁄ ⁄ ⁄ C ⁄ ⁄ ⁄ F ⁄ ⁄ ⁄ C ⁄
Jor- dan's riv - er is chill- y and cold, hal - le - lu - jah!

(C ⁄) C ⁄ ⁄ ⁄ G7 ⁄ ⁄ ⁄ C ⁄ G7 ⁄ C 𝄐
Jor- dan's riv - er is chill- y and cold, hal - le - lu - jah!

Verse 4:

(C ⁄) C ⁄ ⁄ ⁄ C ⁄ ⁄ ⁄ F ⁄ ⁄ ⁄ C ⁄
Mi- chael's boat is a gos - pel boat. hal - le - lu - jah!

(C ⁄) C ⁄ ⁄ ⁄ G7 ⁄ ⁄ ⁄ C ⁄ G7 ⁄ C 𝄐
Mi- chael's boat is a gos - pel boat. hal - le - lu - jah!

The chords used in this song are:

C
G7
F
C7

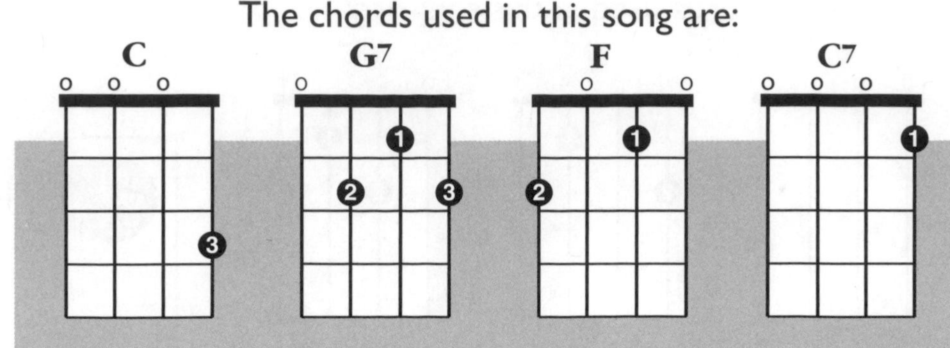

Frankie and Johnny

American Folk Song

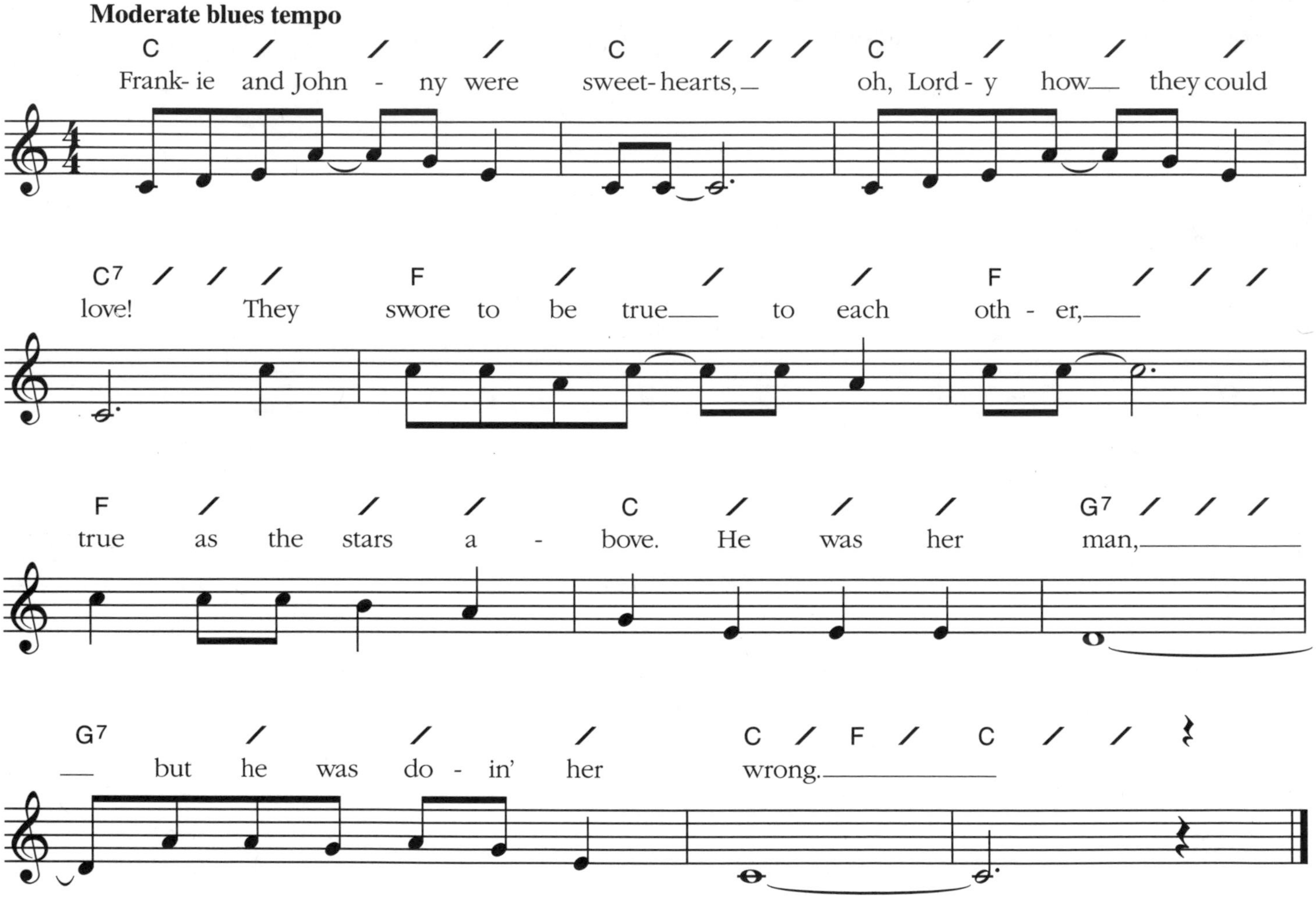

Moderate blues tempo
C / / / C / / / C / / /
Frank- ie and John - ny were sweet- hearts, oh, Lord - y how they could
C7 / / / F / / / F / / /
love! They swore to be true to each oth - er,
F / / / C / / / G7 / / /
true as the stars a - bove. He was her man,
G7 / / / C / F / C / / 𝄽
but he was do - in' her wrong.

MINI MUSIC LESSON: BLUES STRUM

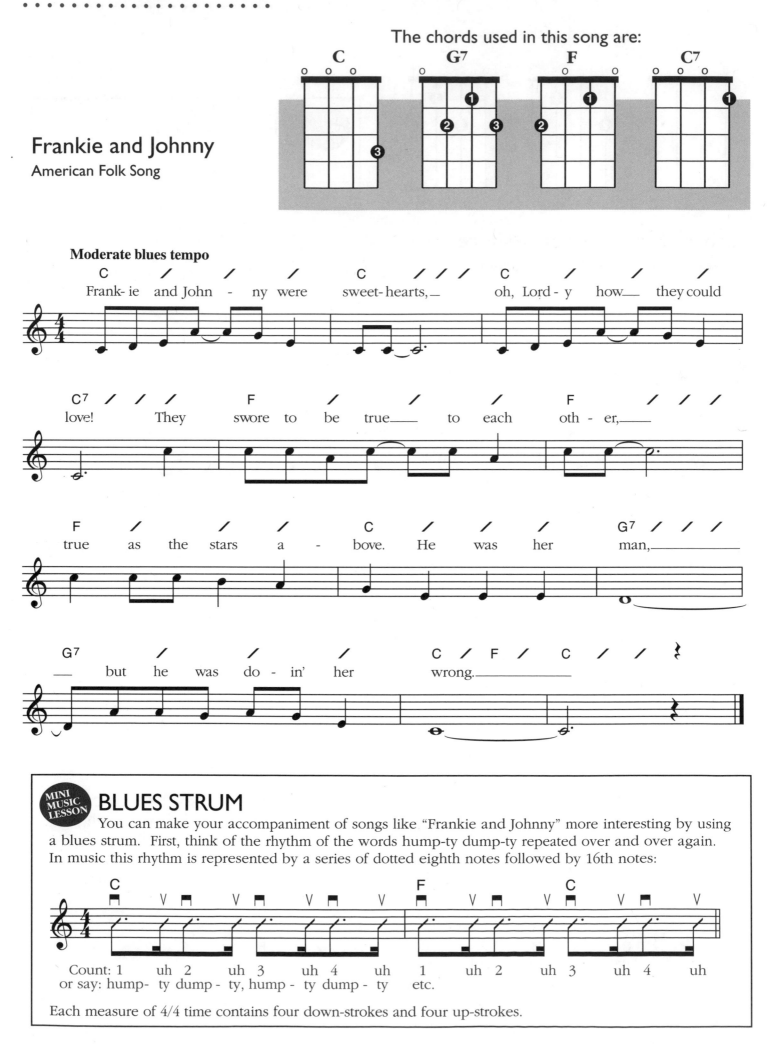

You can make your accompaniment of songs like "Frankie and Johnny" more interesting by using a blues strum. First, think of the rhythm of the words hump-ty dump-ty repeated over and over again. In music this rhythm is represented by a series of dotted eighth notes followed by 16th notes:

C F C

Count: 1 uh 2 uh 3 uh 4 uh 1 uh 2 uh 3 uh 4 uh
or say: hump- ty dump - ty, hump - ty dump - ty etc.

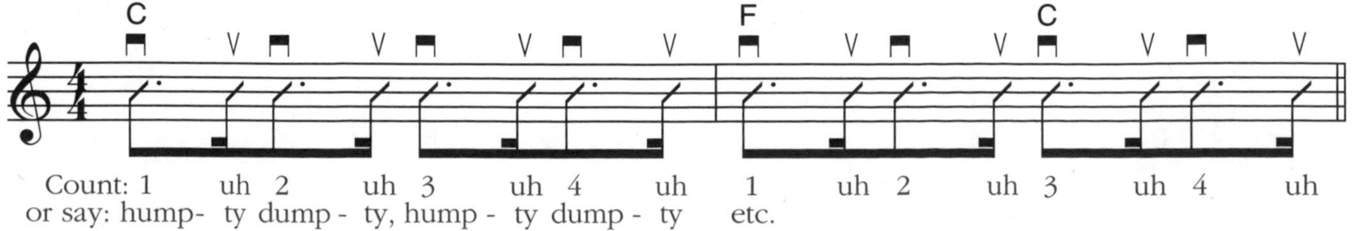

Each measure of 4/4 time contains four down-strokes and four up-strokes.

The chords used in this song are:

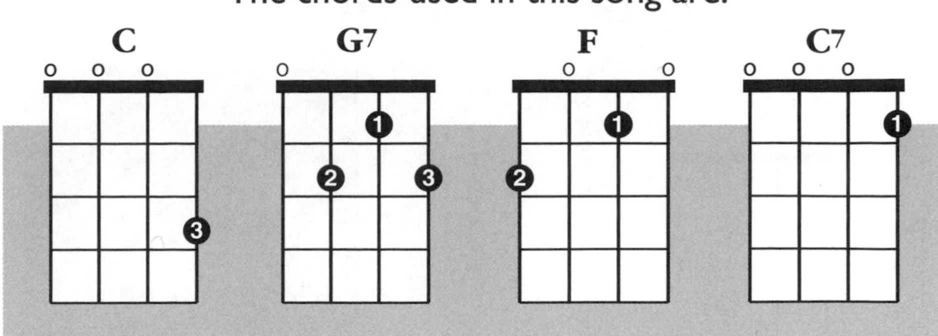

Careless Love

Blues Song

The blues strum you learned on the previous page also works nicely for this song.

Additional Verse

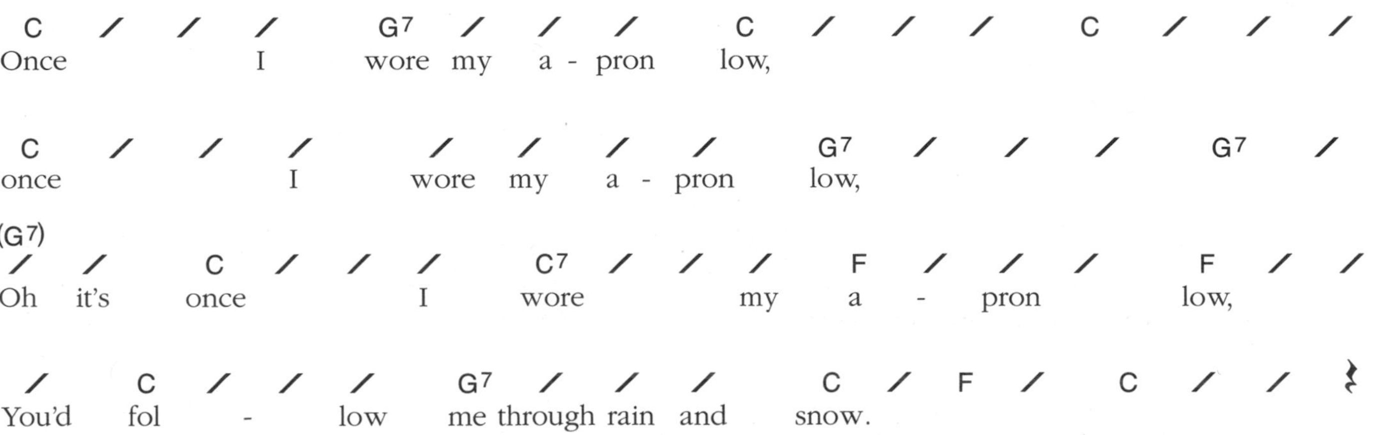

How to Play the G Chord

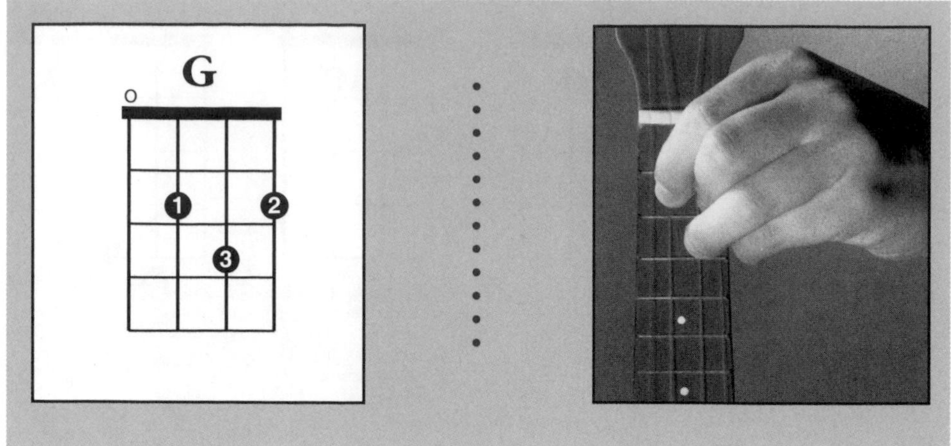

Place ❶, ❷ and ❸ in position, then play one string at a time:

Play all four strings together:

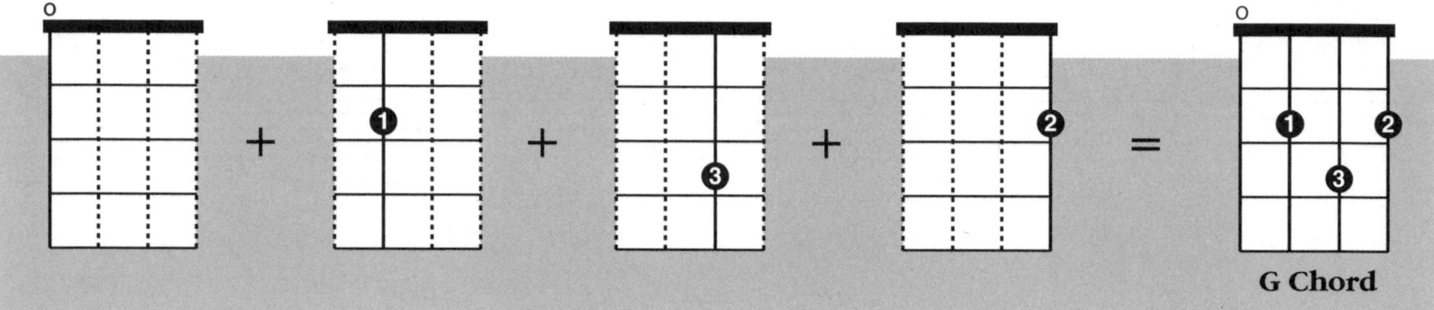

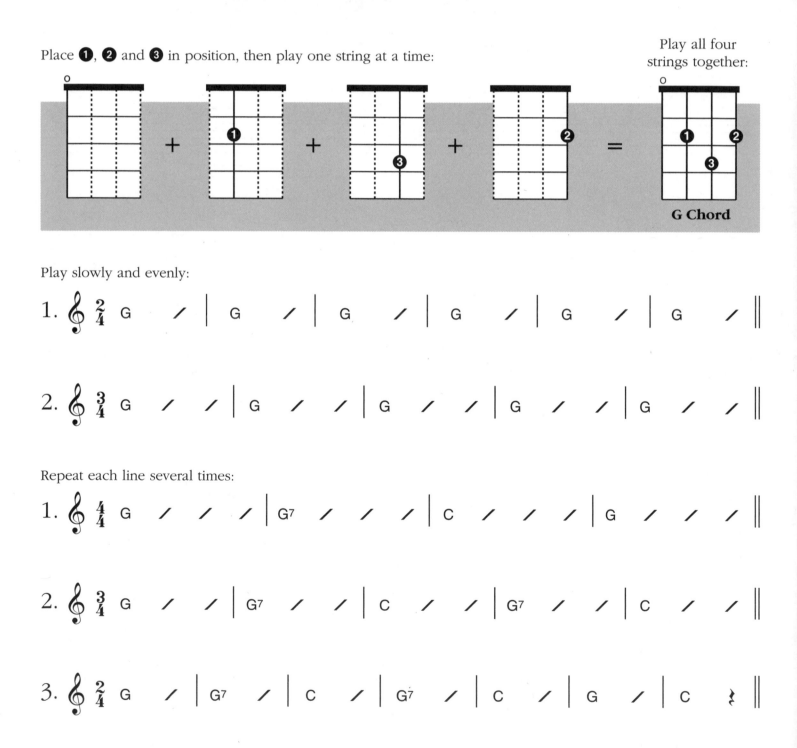

Play slowly and evenly:

1. 2/4 | G / | G / | G / | G / | G / | G / ||

2. 3/4 | G / / | G / / | G / / | G / / | G / / ||

Repeat each line several times:

1. 4/4 | G / / / | G7 / / / | C / / / | G / / / ||

2. 3/4 | G / / | G7 / / | C / / | G7 / / | C / / ||

3. 2/4 | G / | G7 / | C / | G7 / | C / | G / | C 𝄽 ||

How to Play the D7 Chord

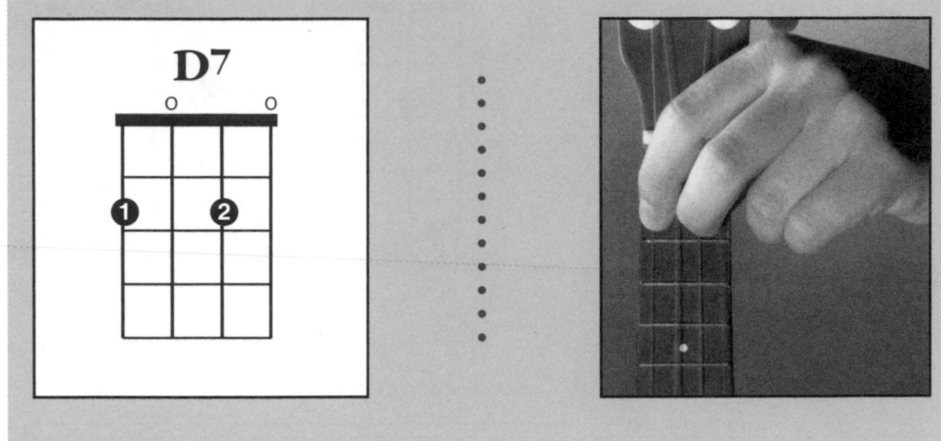

Place ❶ and ❷ in position, then play one string at a time:

Play all four strings together:

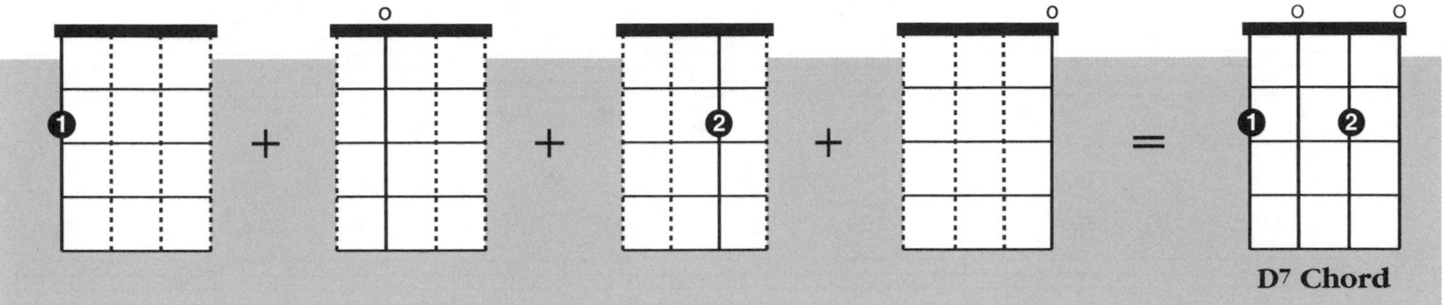

Play slowly and evenly:

1. 2/4 D7 / | D7 / | D7 / | D7 / | D7 / | D7 / ||

2. 3/4 D7 / / | D7 / / | D7 / / | D7 / / | D7 / / ||

Repeat each line several times:

1. 4/4 G / / / | D7 / / / | C / / / | D7 / / / | G ||

2. 3/4 G / / | C / / | D7 / / | C / / | G ||

3. 2/4 G / | G7 / | C / | D7 / | G / | C D7 | G ||

The chords used in this song are:

G
D7
1
2
3
1
2

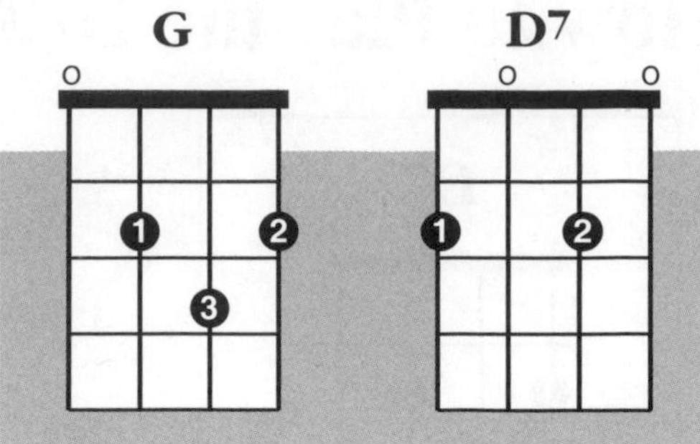

Lolly-Too-Dum

American Mountain Folk Song

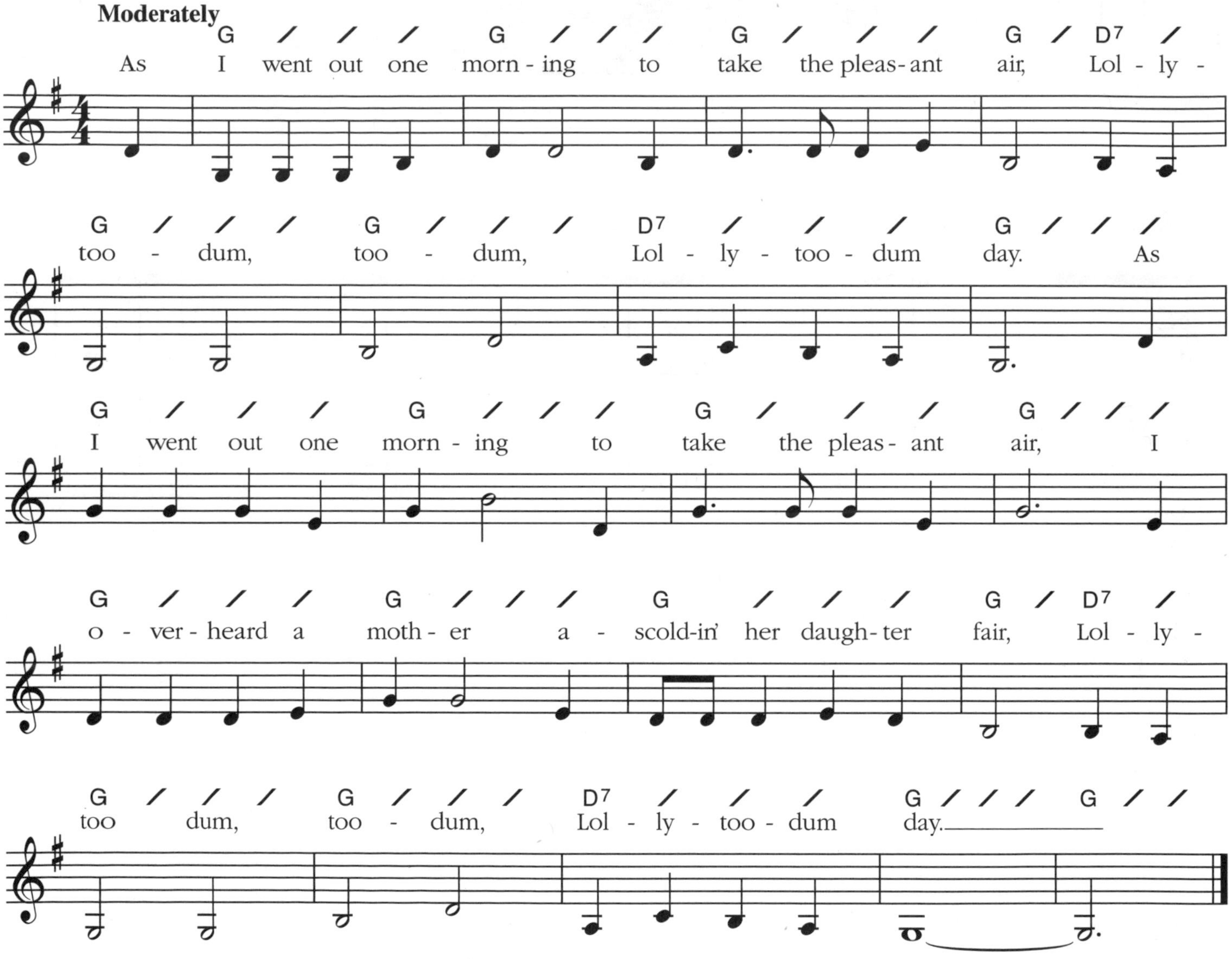

Moderately
G / / / G / / / G / / / G / D7 /
As I went out one morn - ing to take the pleas- ant air, Lol - ly -
G / / / G / / / D7 / / / G / / /
too - dum, too - dum, Lol - ly - too - dum day. As
G / / / G / / / G / / / G / / /
I went out one morn - ing to take the pleas- ant air, I
G / / / G / / / G / / / G / D7 /
o - ver - heard a moth - er a - scold-in' her daugh- ter fair, Lol - ly -
G / / / G / / / D7 / / / G / / / G / /
too dum, too - dum, Lol - ly - too - dum day.

BLUEGRASS STRUM

MINI MUSIC LESSON

You can make your accompaniment of this country favorite more interesting by using a bluegrass strum. This strum breaks up the steady four-beats-to-the-measure with up-strokes on the second and fourth beats. Try the exercise below, and when you can do it smoothly apply it to "Lolly-Too-Dum."

G
D7
G
D7
G
etc.
Count: 1 2 & 3 4 & 1 2 & 3 4 & etc.

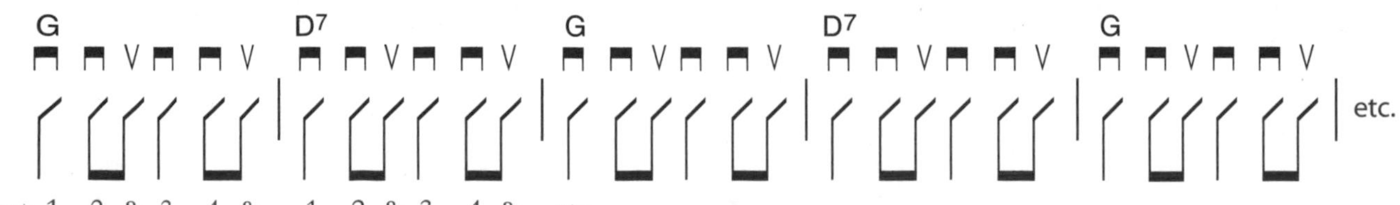

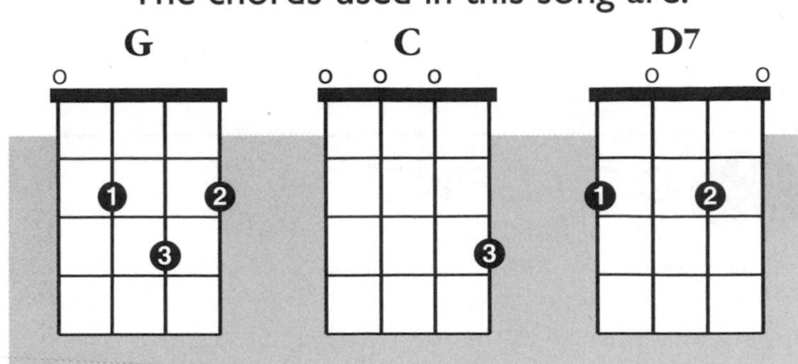

Little Brown Jug

19th Century Vaudeville Song

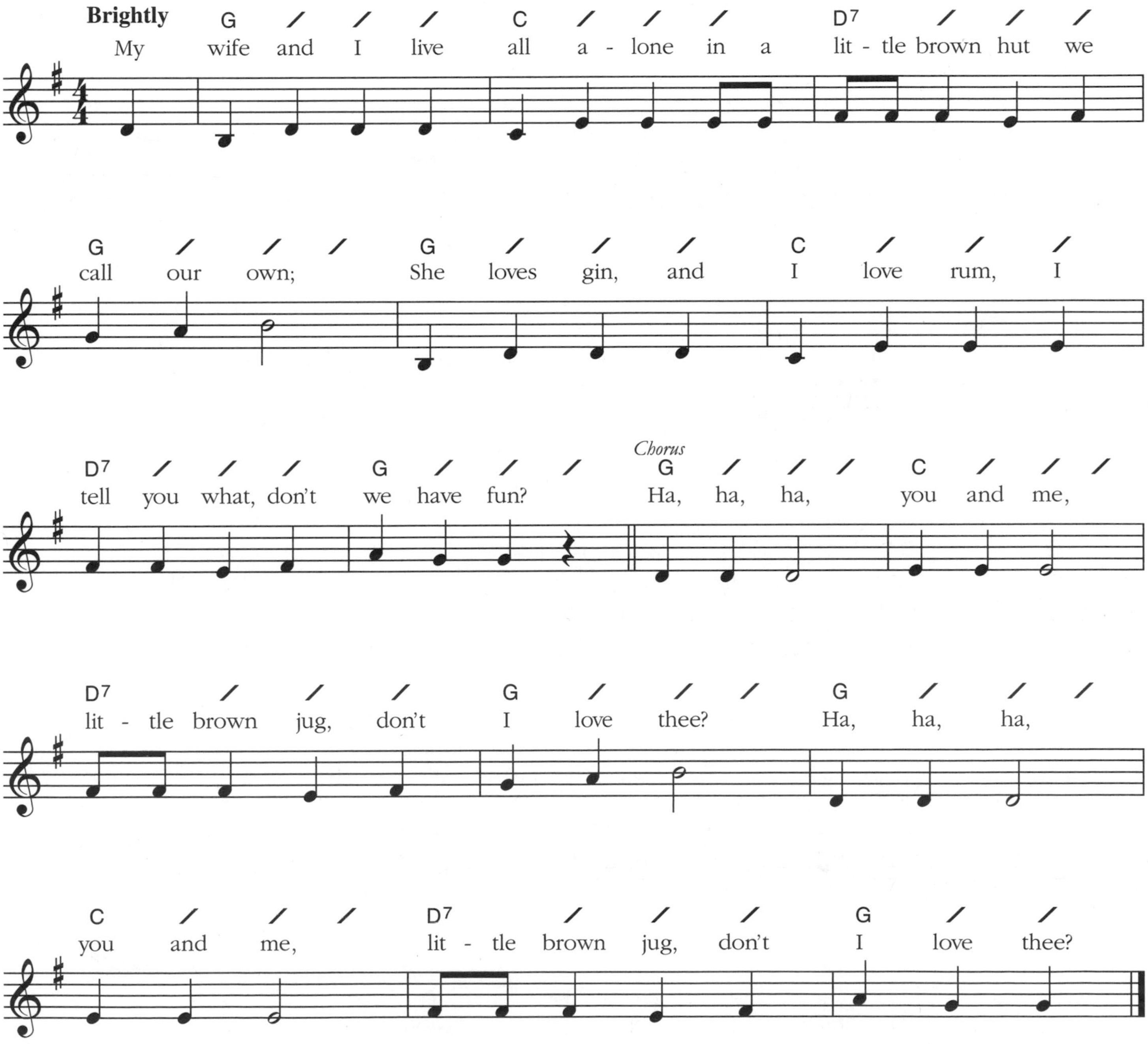

Brightly

G / / / C / / / D7 / / /
My wife and I live all a - lone in a lit - tle brown hut we

G / / / G / / / C / / /
call our own; She loves gin, and I love rum, I

D7 / / / G / / /
tell you what, don't we have fun?

Chorus

G / / / C / / /
Ha, ha, ha, you and me,

D7 / / / G / / / G / / /
lit - tle brown jug, don't I love thee? Ha, ha, ha,

C / / / D7 / / / G / /
you and me, lit - tle brown jug, don't I love thee?

The bluegrass strum you learned on the previous page works nicely on this song also.

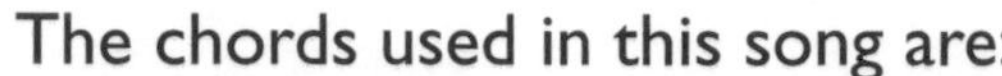

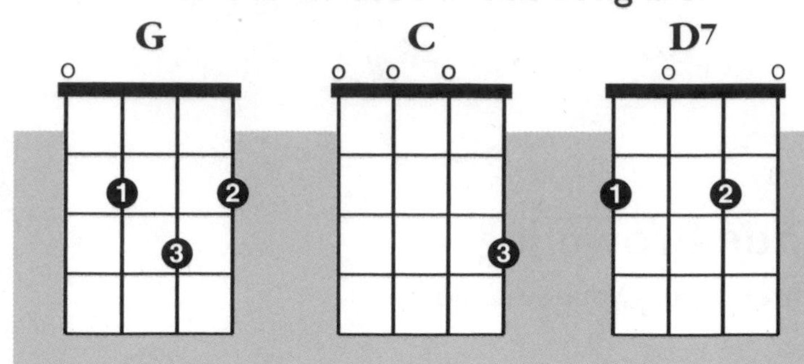

The chords used in this song are:

G
C
D7

MINI MUSIC LESSON

D.C. AL FINE

D.C. al Fine stands for the Italian expression "Da capo al fine" (dah CAH-po al FEE-nay). It means to go back to the beginning of the song and play as far as the word "Fine" (end).

Gimme That Old-Time Religion

Traditional Gospel Song

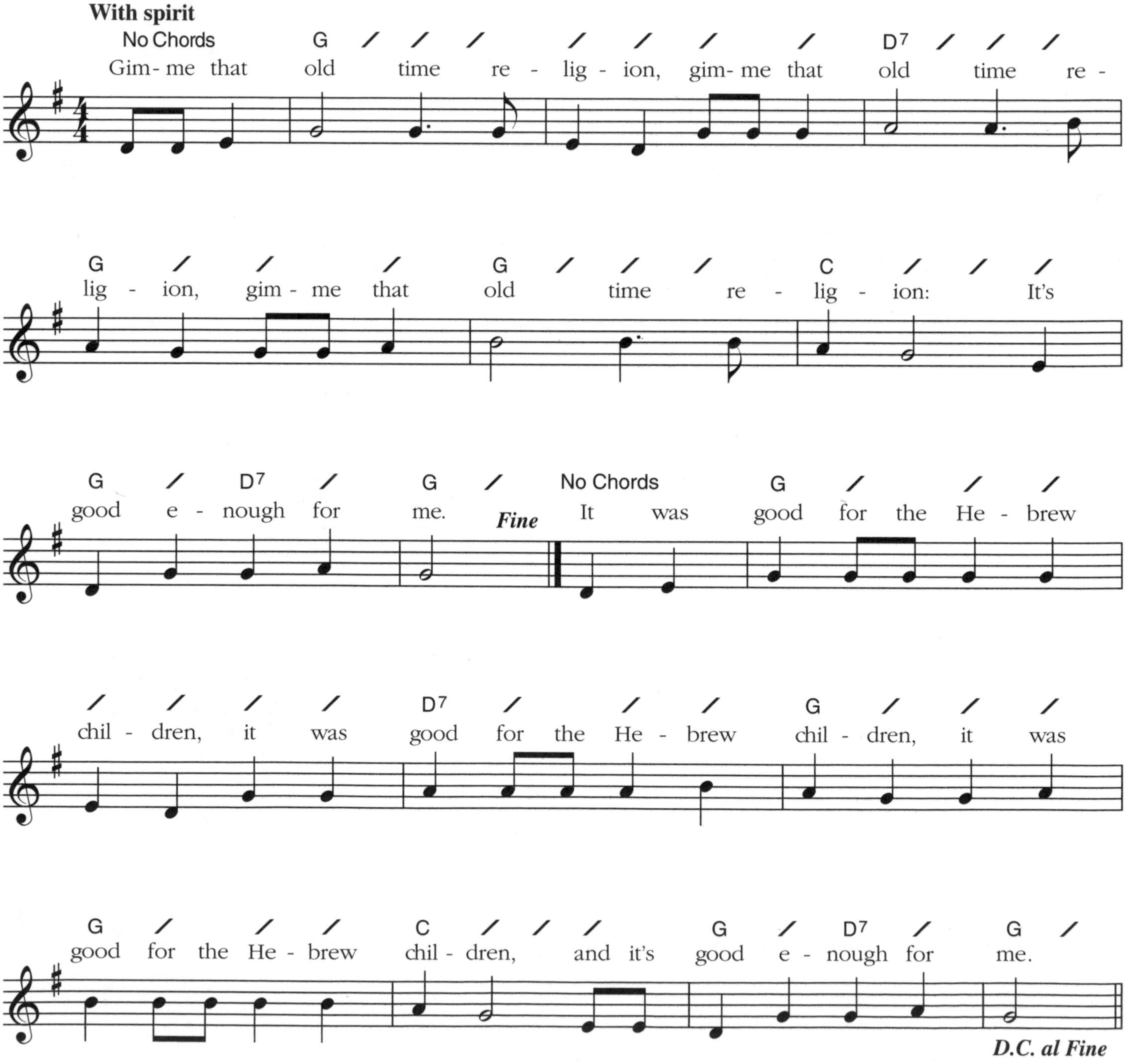

With spirit
No Chords G D7
Gim-me that old time re-lig-ion, gim-me that old time re-
G G C
lig-ion, gim-me that old time re-lig-ion: It's
G D7 G No Chords G
good e-nough for me. Fine It was good for the He-brew
D7 G
chil-dren, it was good for the He-brew chil-dren, it was
G C G D7 G
good for the He-brew chil-dren, and it's good e-nough for me.
D.C. al Fine

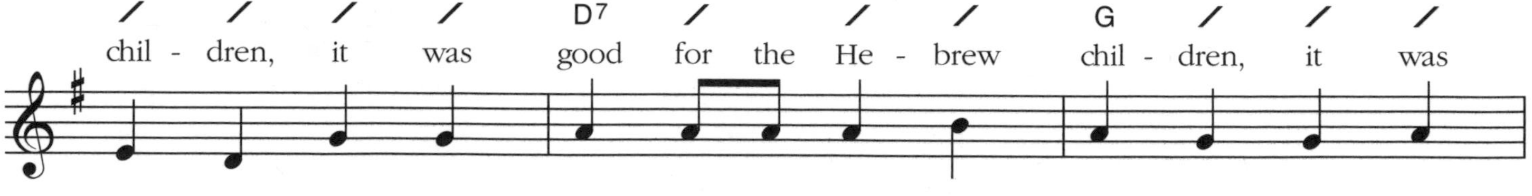

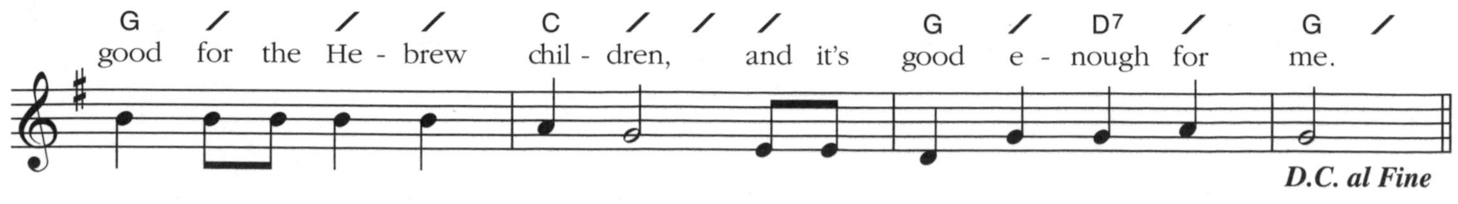

The chords used in this song are:

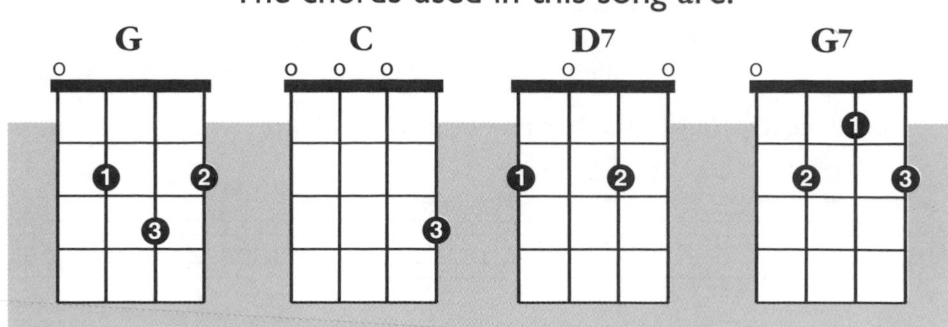

When the Saints Go Marching In

Traditional Gospel Song

Moderate Dixieland jazz feel

No Chords G / / / G / / / G / / / G / / /
Oh when the saints go march - ing in, Oh when the

G / / / G / / / D7 / / / D7 / / /
saints go march - ing in, Oh Lord, I

G / / / G7 / / / C / / / C / / /
want to be in that num - ber, when the

G / / / C / D7 / G / C / G
saints go march - ing in.

Verse 2:

No chords G / / / G / / / G / / /
And when that sun be - gins to shine,

G / / / G / / / G / / / D7 / / /
Oh when that sun be - gins to shine,

D7 / / / G / / / G7 / / / C / / /
Oh Lord, I want to be in that num - ber,

C / / / G / / / C / D7 / G / C / G
When that sun be - gins to shine.

THE CALYPSO STRUM

MINI MUSIC LESSON

The calypso strum is used to accompany Caribbean songs like "Mary Ann," "Jamaica Farewell" and "The Sloop John B." The rhythm is a little tricky, so make sure you can play the exercises on this page before trying the songs.

1. Play a steady four-to-the-bar pattern on a D chord. Use only down-strokes.

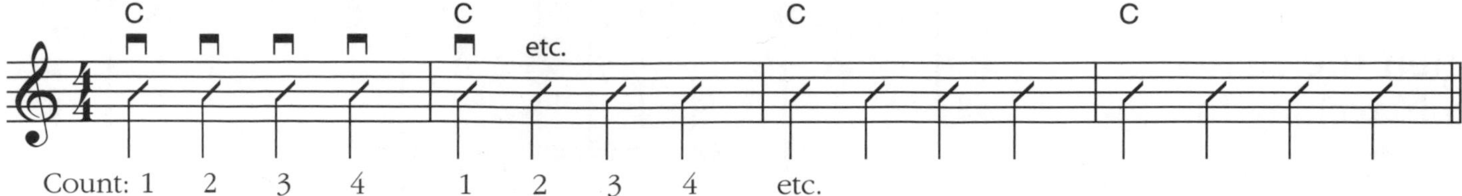

2. Now add an up-stroke after each down-stroke. Notice how the count has changed.

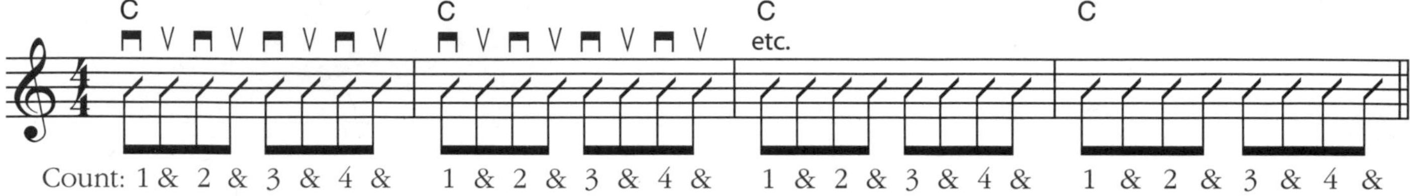

3. Now leave out the down stroke on 3 and replace it with silence. Notice that you now have two up-strokes in a row on the "and" of 2 and the "and" of 3.

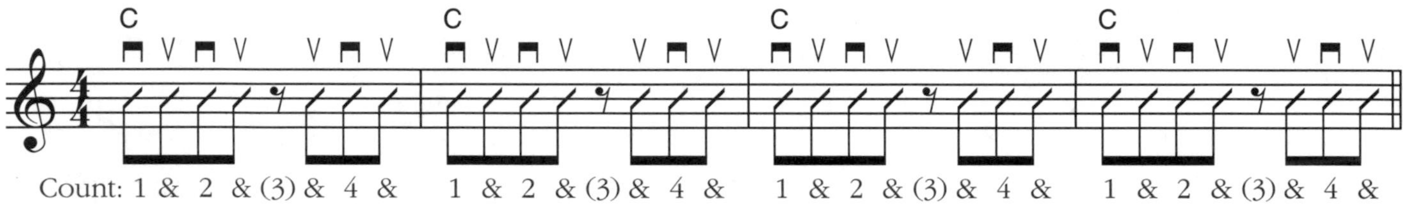

This whole pattern represents one measure of the calypso strum. As soon as you can do it without missing a beat, try "Mary Ann."

Mary Ann

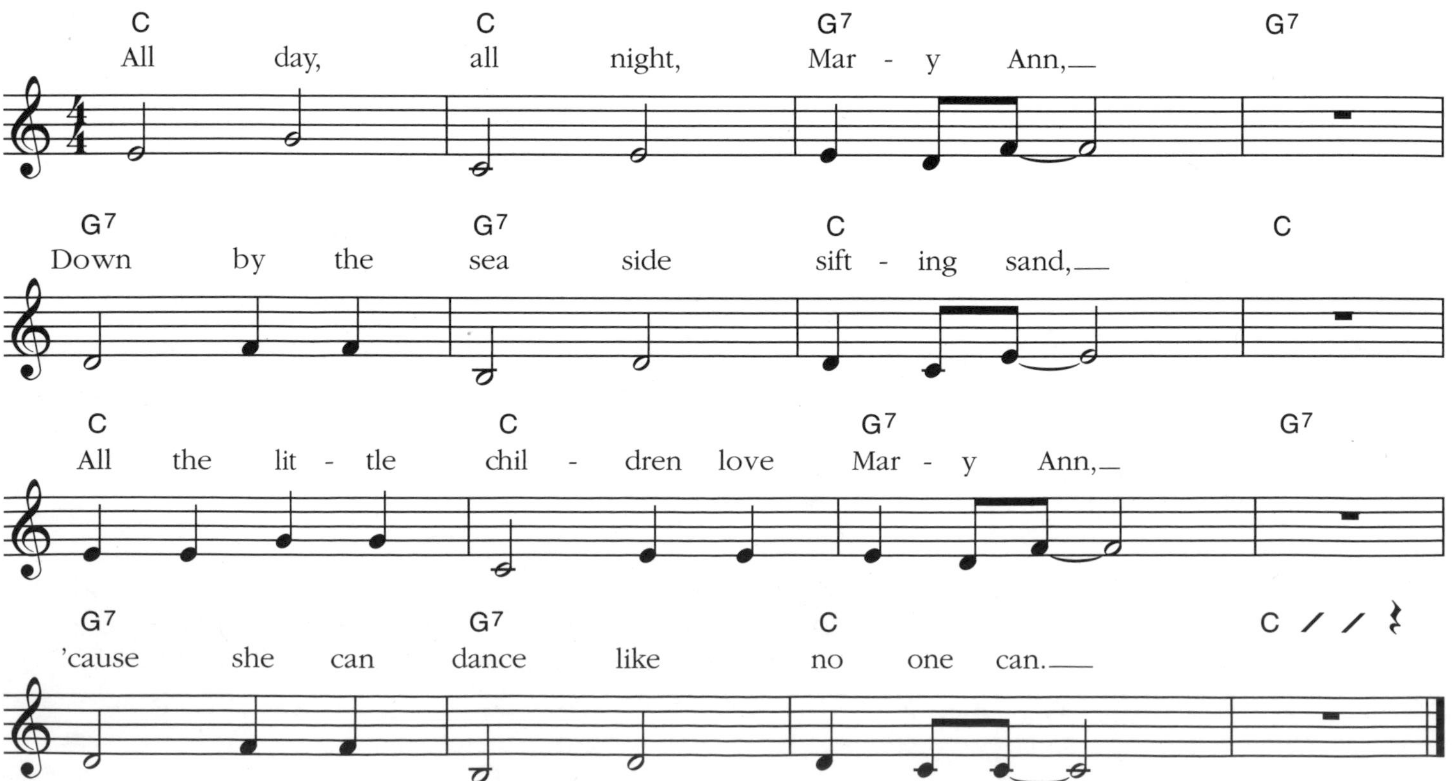

The chords used in this song are:

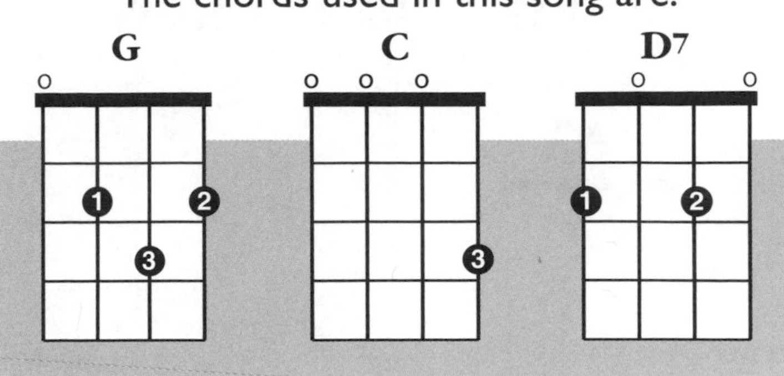

The Sloop John B.

Calypso Song

Start this song with the calypso strum to get into the rhythm of it. Then start singing.

Moderately

G C D7 G We

G G G G
sailed on __ the sloop "John B.," my grand - fa - ther and me, We

G G D7 D7
left Nas - sau Town one morn - ing at dawn. __ I want __ to go

G G C C
home, __ I want __ to go home, __ Oh, I

G D7 G G
feel so break __ up I want __ to go home. __

How to Play the A7 Chord

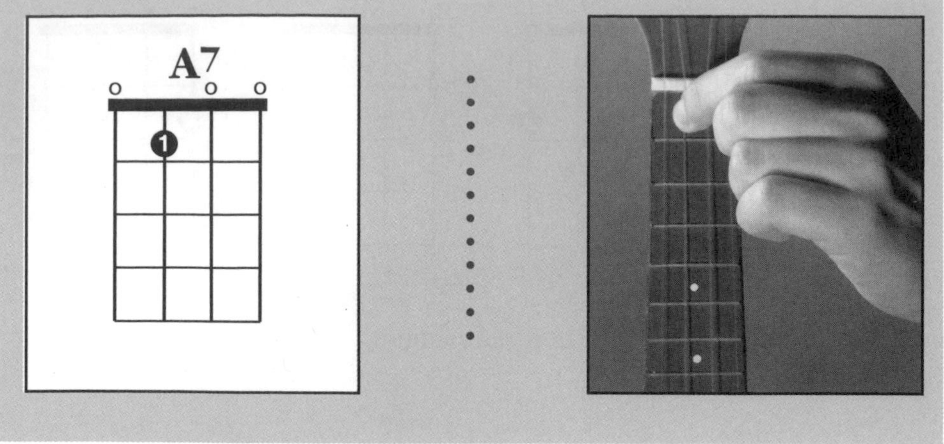

Place ❶ in position, then play one string at a time:

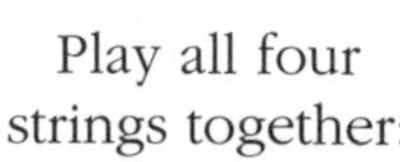

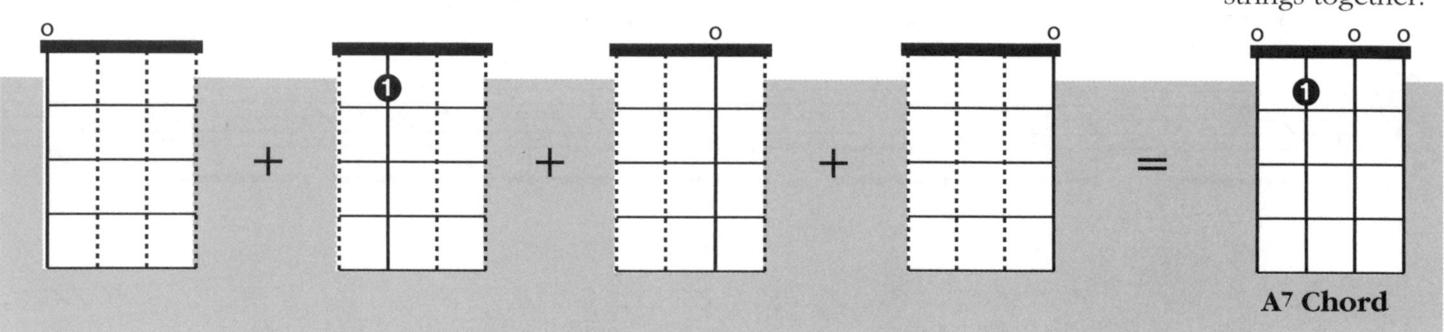

How to Play the D Minor Chord

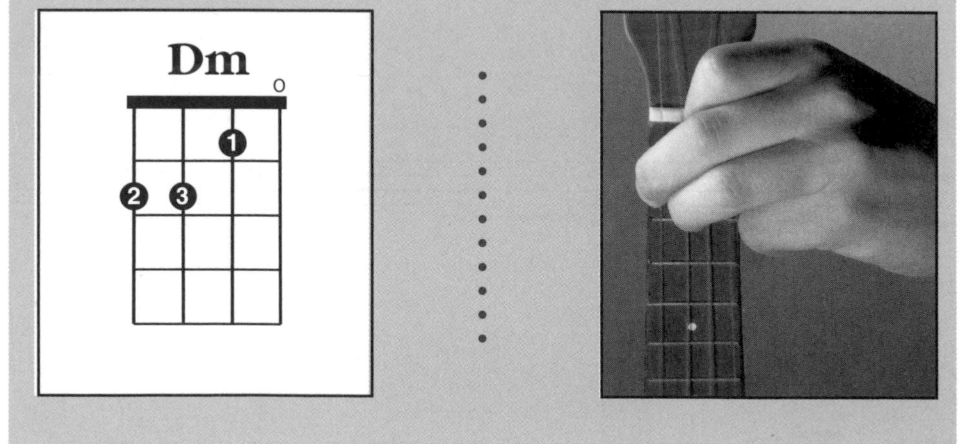

Minor Chords

You have already learned chords in two different categories, major chords (represented by a capital letter), and seventh chords (represented by a capital letter followed by the number 7). Another important category of chords is minor chords. These chords are represented by a capital letter followed by a small m. (Some editions use "min." to represent minor chords.)

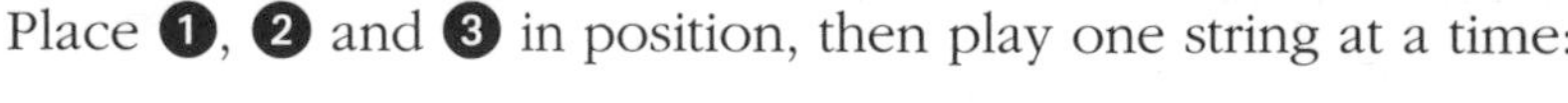

Play all four strings together:

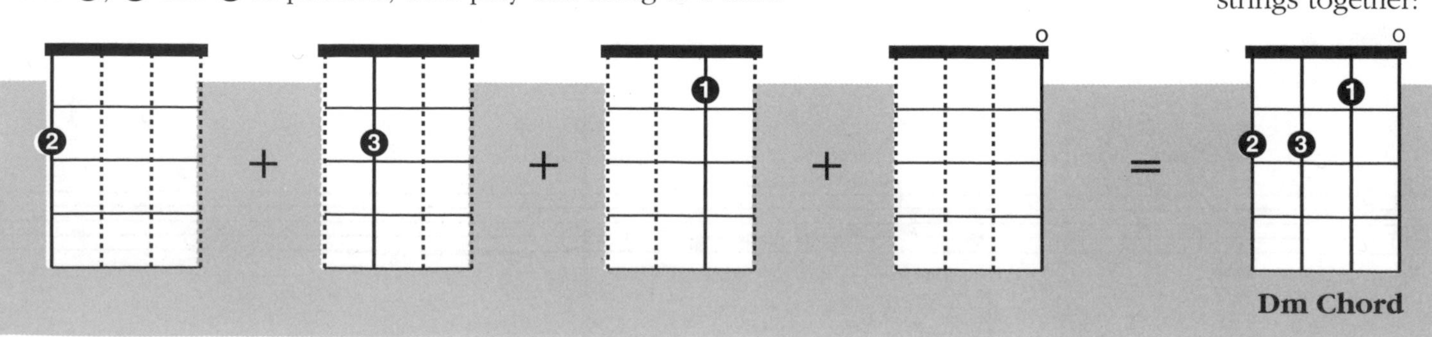

The chords used in this song are:

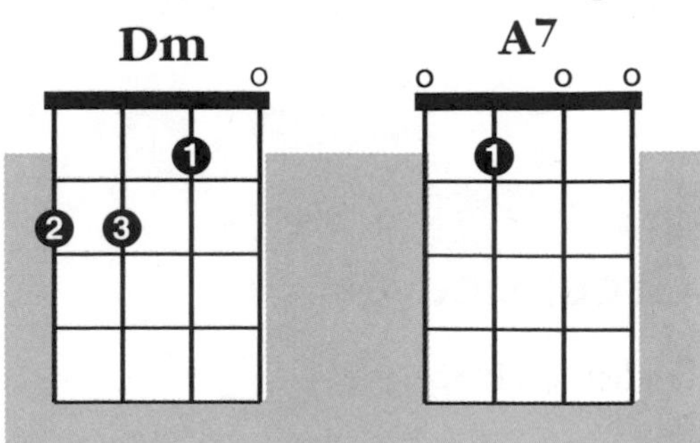

Joshua Fought the Battle of Jericho

Traditional Gospel Song

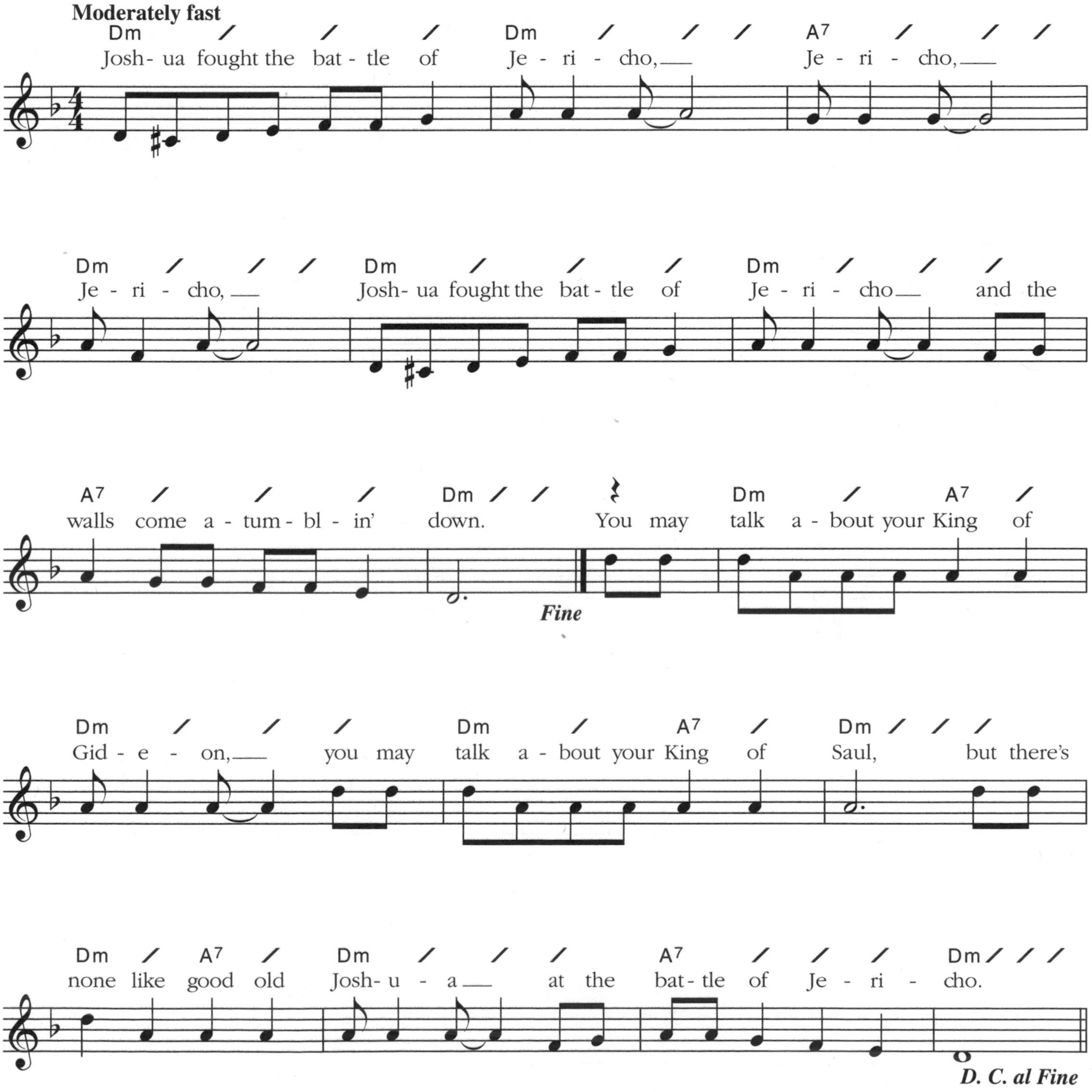

Moderately fast

Dm / / / Dm / / / A7 / / /
Josh- ua fought the bat - tle of Je - ri - cho, Je - ri - cho,

Dm / / / Dm / / / Dm / / /
Je - ri - cho, Josh- ua fought the bat - tle of Je - ri - cho and the

A7 / / / Dm / / Dm / A7 /
walls come a - tum - bl - in' down. You may talk a - bout your King of

Fine

Dm / / / Dm / A7 / Dm / / /
Gid - e - on, you may talk a - bout your King of Saul, but there's

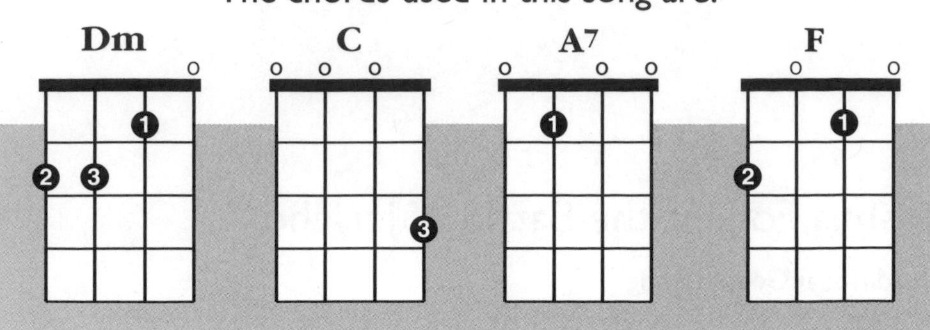

Greensleeves

English Folk Song

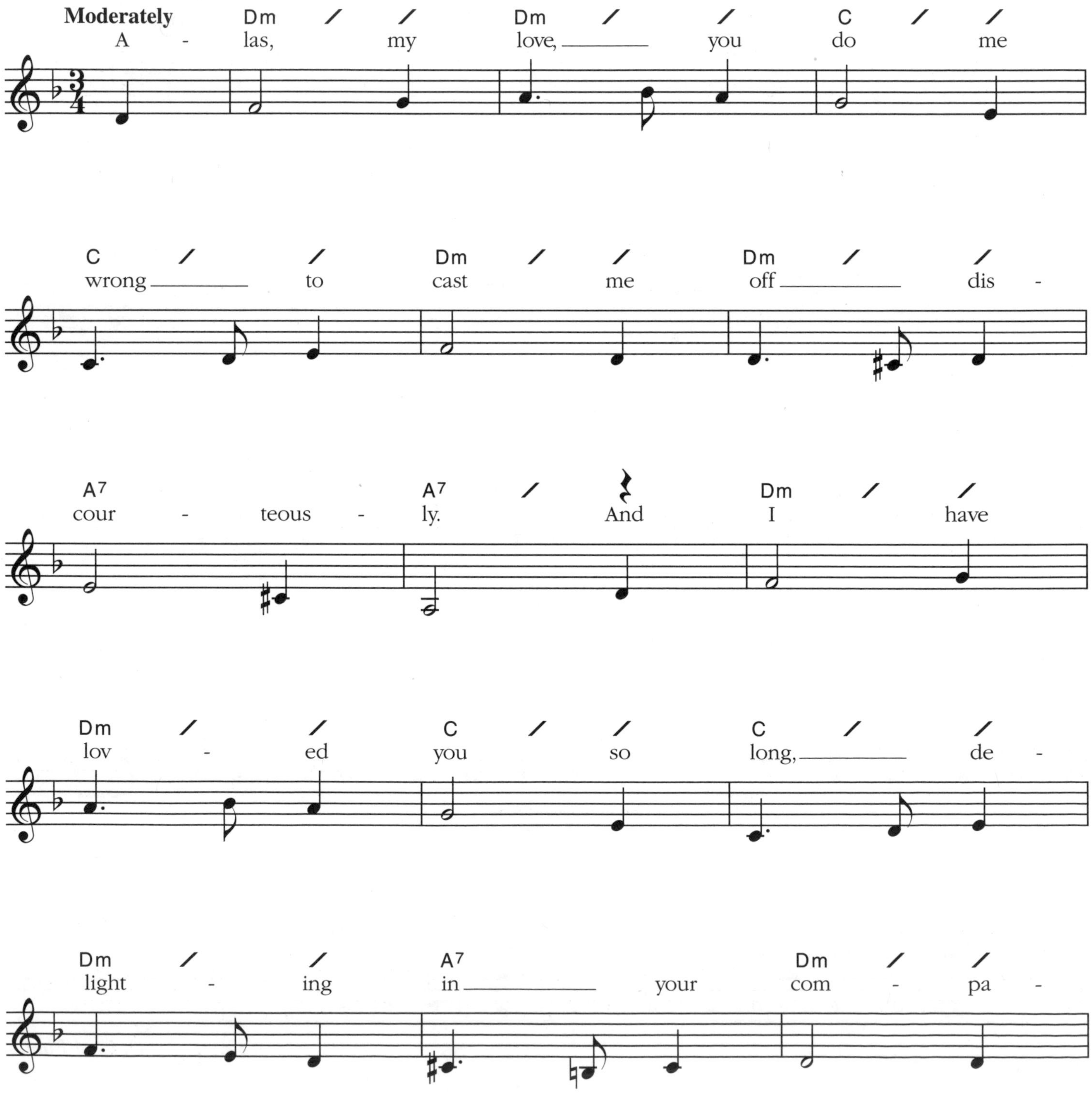

Moderately

Dm / / Dm / / C / /
A - las, my love, you do me

C / / Dm / / Dm / /
wrong to cast me off dis -

A7 A7 / Dm / /
cour - teous - ly. And I have

Dm / / C / / C / /
lov - ed you so long, de -

Dm F F
ny. Green - sleeves was
C C Dm
all my joy, Green -
Dm A7 A7
sleeves was my de - light,
F F C
Green - sleeves my heart of
C Dm
gold, And who but my
A7 Dm Dm
La - dy Green - sleeves?

The chords used in this song are:

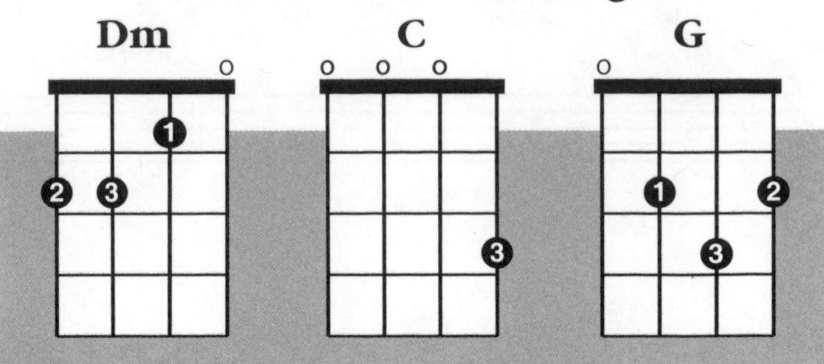

Scarborough Fair

English Folk Song

Moderately slow

Dm / / Dm / / C / /
Are you goin' to Scar - bo - rough

Dm / / Dm / / Dm / / Dm / /
Fair? Pars - ley, sage, rose -

G / / Dm / / Dm / /
ma - ry and thyme; Re -

Dm / / Dm / / Dm / /
mem - ber me to one who lives

C / / C / / Dm / /
there, For once she

C / / C / / Dm / / Dm
was a true love of mine.

How to Play the G Minor Chord

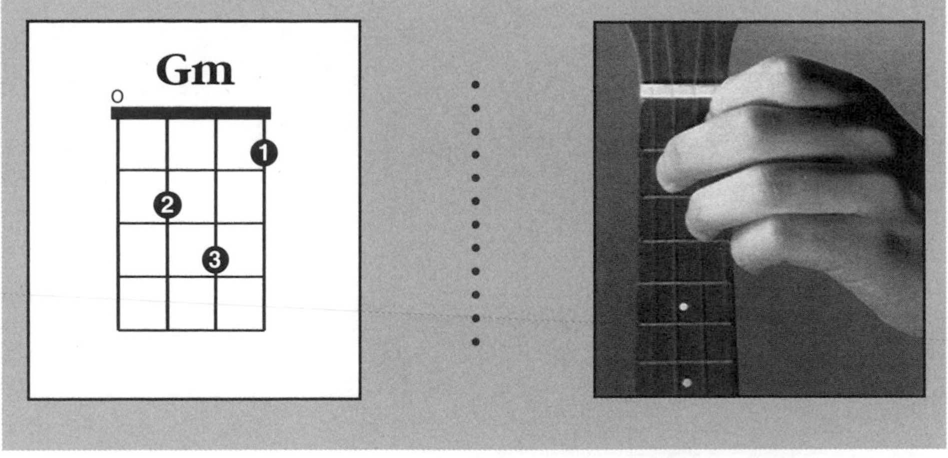
Gm

Place ❶, ❷ and ❸ in position, then play one string at a time:

Play all four strings together:

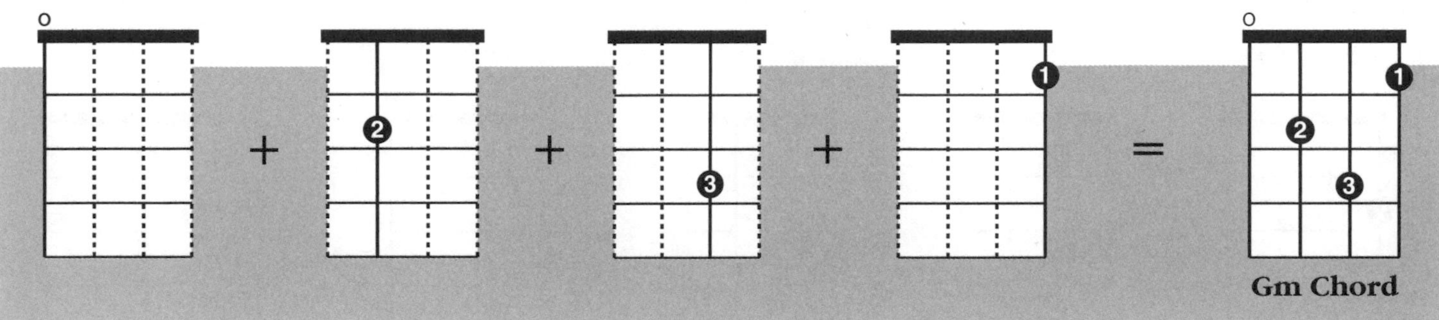
Gm Chord

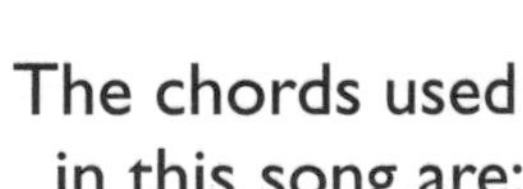
The chords used
in this song are:

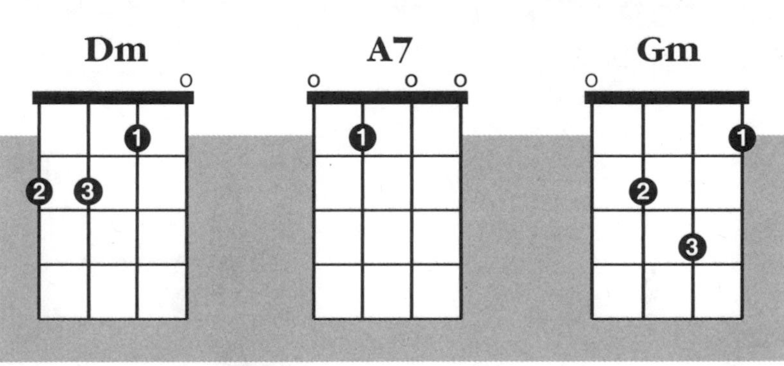
Dm
A7
Gm

Go Down, Moses

American Spiritual

Slowly
Dm A7 Dm A7 Dm
When Is - rael was in E - gypt land, let my peo - ple go. Op -
Dm A7 Dm A7 Dm
pressed so hard they could not stand, let my peo - ple go.
Dm Gm A7 Dm
Go down, Mo - ses, way down in E - gypt land.
Dm Dm A7 Dm
Tell old Pha - raoh, "Let my peo - ple go."

How to Play the A Chord

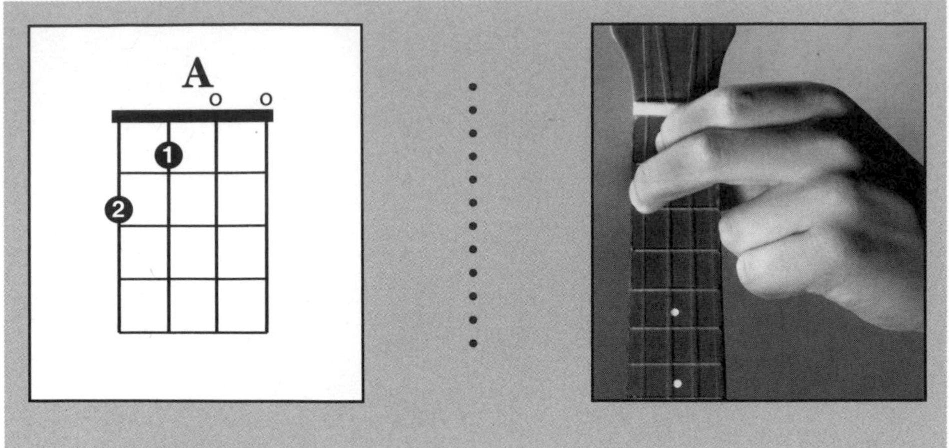
A

Place ❶ and ❷ in position, then play one string at a time:

Play all four strings together:

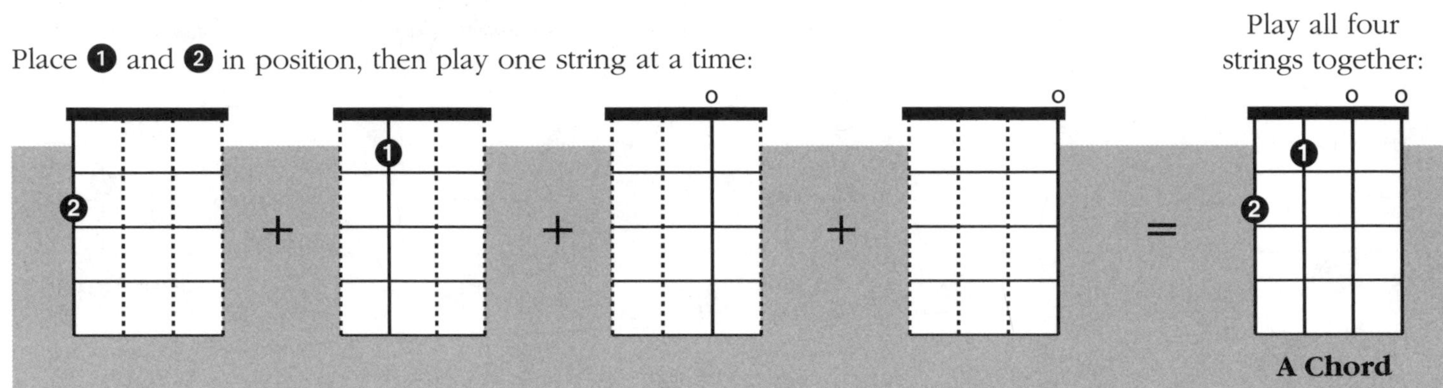
A Chord

The chords used in this song are:

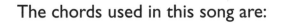

Hava Nagila

Israeli Folk Dance

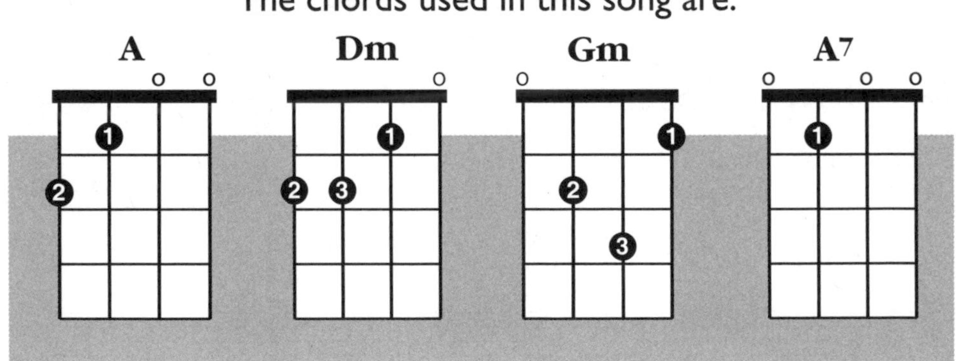
A
Dm
Gm
A7

Moderately, with spirit
A A A A
Be - lieve in peo - ple, be - lieve in peo - ple,
Dm Dm A Gm A
be - lieve in peo - ple, all men are e - qual.

A / / / A / / / Gm / / / Gm / / /
Fear not his col - or of skin, fear not his re - li - gion,
Gm / / / Gm / / / A / Gm / A / / / Dm / / / Dm / / /
fear not his place of birth, all men are e - qual. All men!
Dm / / / Dm / / / Dm / / / Dm / / /
All men e - qual! O - pen your heart, for - get old teach - ings.
Dm / / / Dm / / / A7 / / /
Be - lieve in truth, the myths are gone now. View ev - 'ry - one as
A7 / / / A7 / / / A7 / / /
a whole per - son, o - ver - come fear e - volved through ha - tred,
A / / A / / A7 / / / A7 / / /
trust in your heart! Strength - en with love! Be - lieve in all the peo - ple
Dm / / / Dm / / / Dm / A7 / Dm Dm
now! Now! Now! Now!

The chords used in this song are:

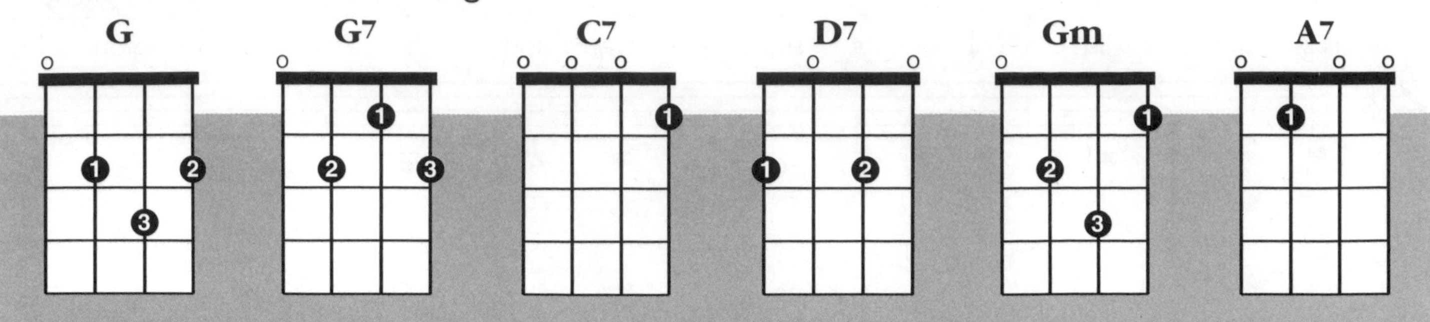

St. Louis Blues

W.C. Handy

Moderately

G / / / D7 / / / G / / / G7 / / /
I hate to see__ the eve-nin' sun go down,__

C7 / / / C7 / / / G / / / G / / /
Hate to see__ the eve-nin' sun go down,__

D7 / / / C7 / / / G / C7 / G / D7 /
'cause__ my ba-by, he done left__ this town.__

G / / / C7 / / / G / / / G7 / / /
Feel-in' to-mor-row like__ I feel to-day,__

C7 / / / C7 / / / G / / / G / / /
Feel to-mor-row like__ I feel to-day,__

D7 / / / C7 / / / G / C / G / D7 /
I'll pack my trunk__ an' make my get a-way.__ St. Lou-is

Gm Gm D7 D7
wo - man, with her dia - mond rings, pulls that
D7 D7 Gm Gm
man a - round by her a - pron strings. If it
Gm Gm D7 D7
weren't for pow - der an' for store - bought hair, the
D7 D7 G A7 D7
man I love would not gone no - where. Got the
G G G
St. Lou - is blues just blue as I can be,
G7 C7 C7
that man got a heart like a rock cast in the
G G D7
sea Or else he would - n't
D7 G C7 G7
gone so far from me.

How to Play the C Diminished Chord

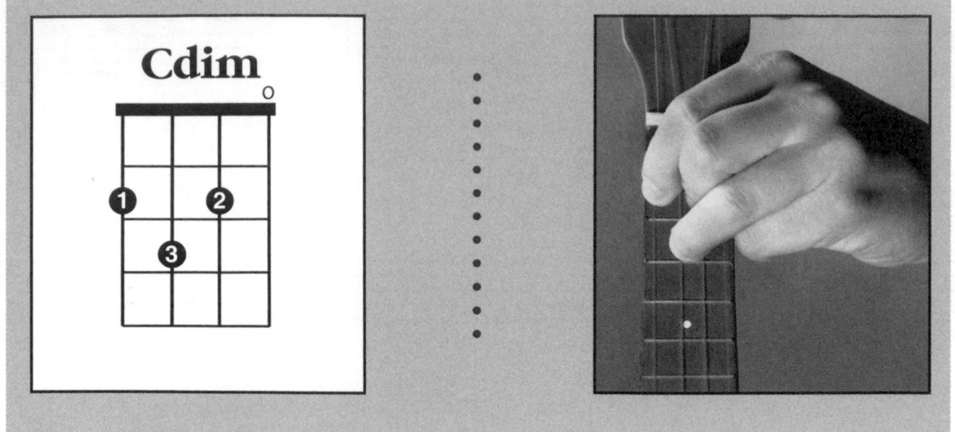

Diminished Chord

Alexander's Ragtime Band introduces a new type of chord called a diminished chord. This is usually abbreviated as "dim." Although diminished chords are rarely used in folk music, they are quite common in popular music, jazz and ragtime. Make sure you understand the fingering of the diminished chord before playing the song.

Place ❶, ❷ and ❸ in position, then play one string at a time:

Play all four strings together:

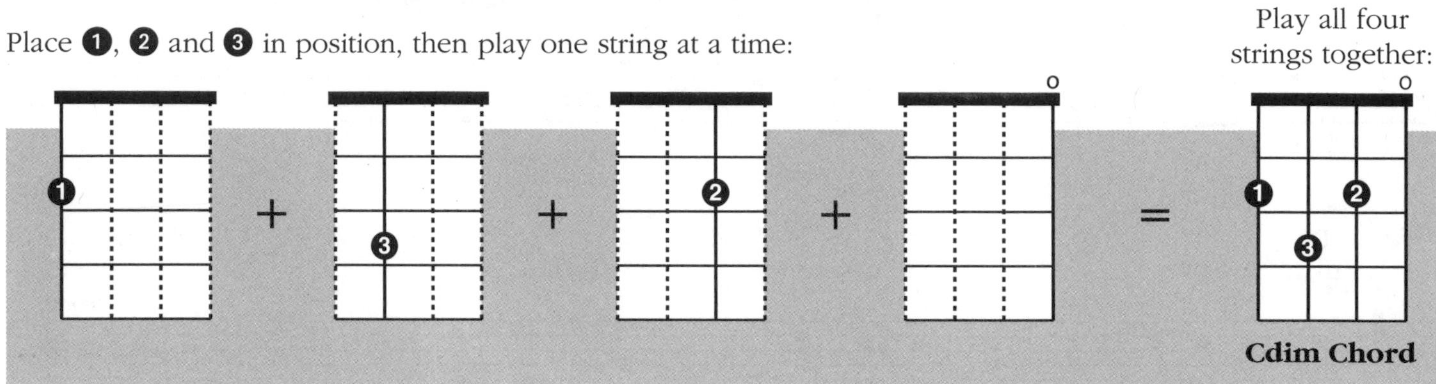

The chords used in this song are:

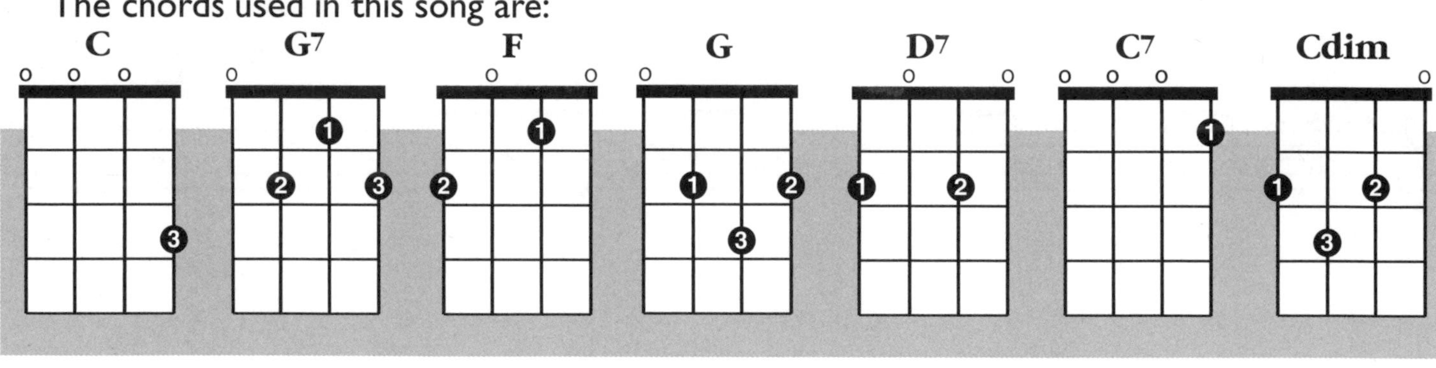

Alexander's Ragtime Band

American Ragtime Song

Irving Berlin

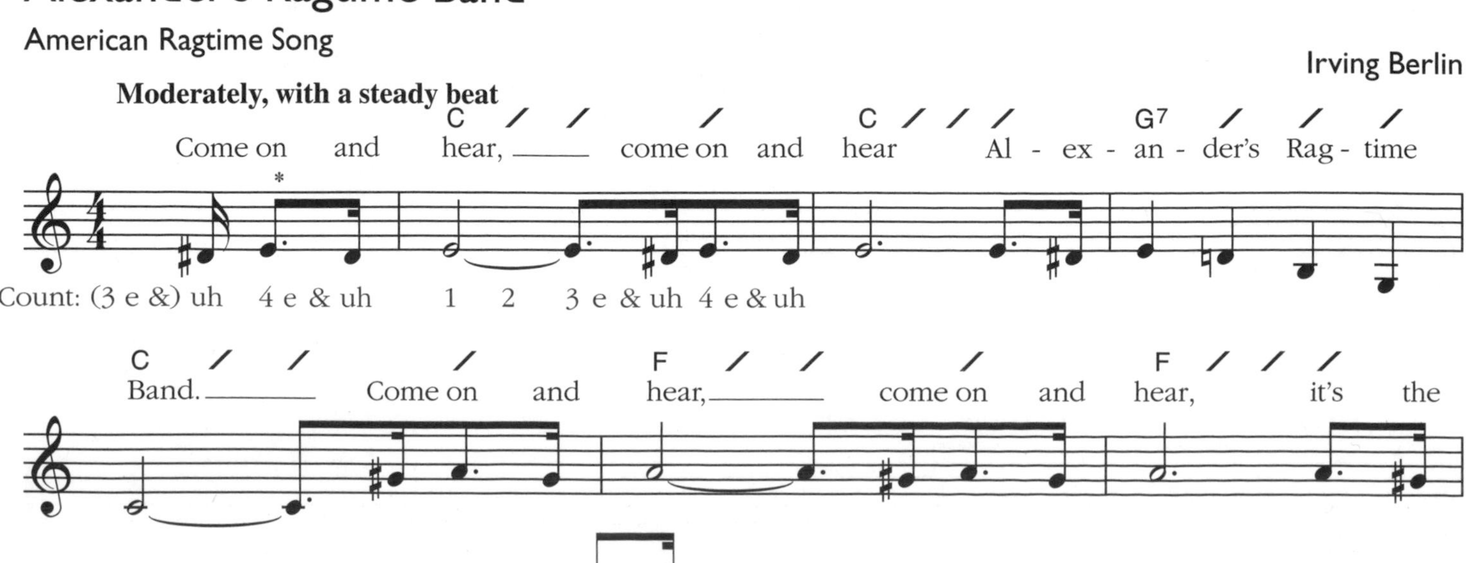

*The dotted eighth-sixteenth rhythm = *Count:* 1 e & uh

F / / / F / / / C / / /
best band in the land. They can play a bu - gle call like you
C / / / C / / / C / / /
nev - er heard be - fore, so nat - u - ral that you want to go to war;
G / / / D7 / / / G / / / G7 / / /
That's just the best - est band what am, hon - ey lamb. Come on a -
C / / / C / / / G7 / / /
long, come on a - long, let me take you by the
C / / / F / / / F / / /
hand up to the man, up to the man, who's the
F / / / F / / / C / / / C7 / / /
lead - er of the band. And if you care to hear the Swan - ee Riv - er
F / / / Cdim / / / C / / /
played in rag - time, come on and hear, come on and
C / / / G7 / / / C / /
hear, Al - ex - an - der's Rag - time Band.

MINI MUSIC LESSON

March Strum

Bright, march-like songs like "The Yankee Doodle Boy" (otherwise known as "I'm a Yankee Doodle Dandy") can be improved by using a march strum to accompany them. This consists of putting a fast up-stroke on the second beat of the measure:

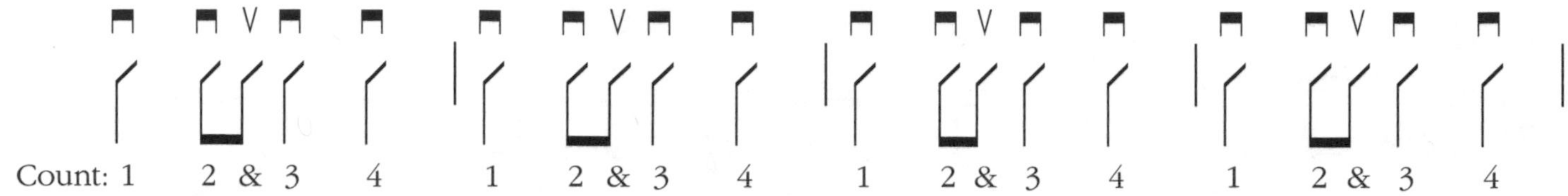

This effect is particularly good when used to fill in places in the melody where there isn't much motion. We've marked these places with a bracket.

The chords used in this song are:

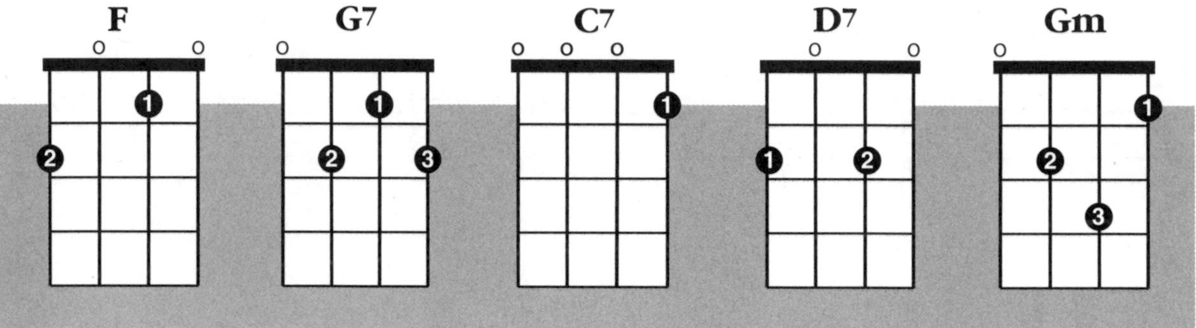

The Yankee Doodle Boy

(I'm a Yankee Doodle Dandy)

Words and Music by George M. Cohan

D7 D7 Gm D7 Gm
real live neph- ew of my Un - cle Sam,

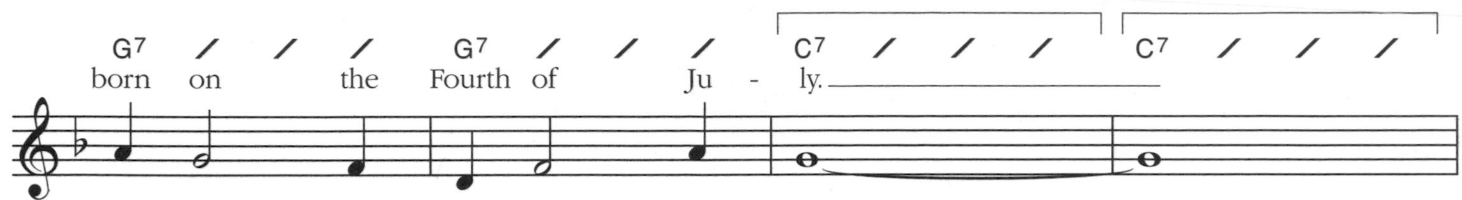
G7 G7 C7 C7
born on the Fourth of Ju - ly.

F F G7 G7
I've a yan - kee doo - dle sweet - heart,

C7 C7 F F
she's my yan - kee doo - dle joy.

F F F F
Yan - kee Doo - dle went to Lon - don just to ride the pon - ies,

G7 C7 F
I am that yan - kee doo - dle boy.

How to Play the B♭ Chord

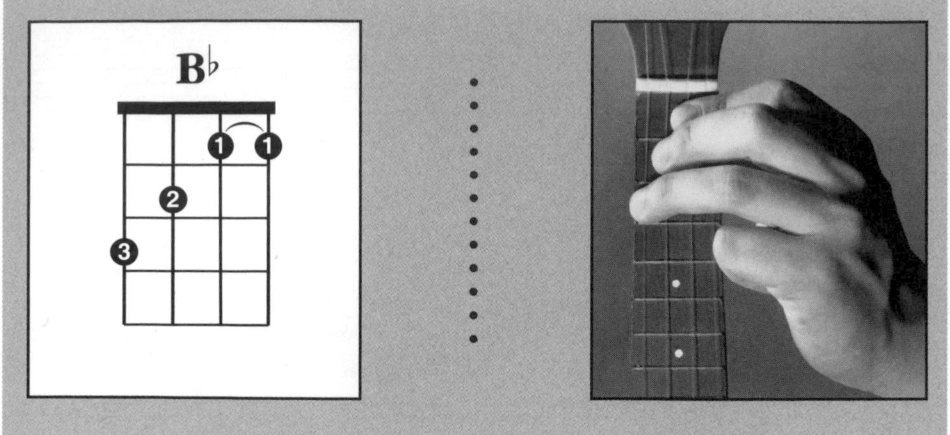

Notice that the first finger covers the first and second strings. Make sure you press hard enough to make both strings sound clear.

As discussed on page 7, the flat sign ♭ lowers the pitch of a note a half step, which on the ukulele is one fret. If this chord were fingered exactly as shown but one fret higher, it would be a B chord.

Place ❶, ❷ and ❸ in position, then play one string at a time:

Play all four strings together:

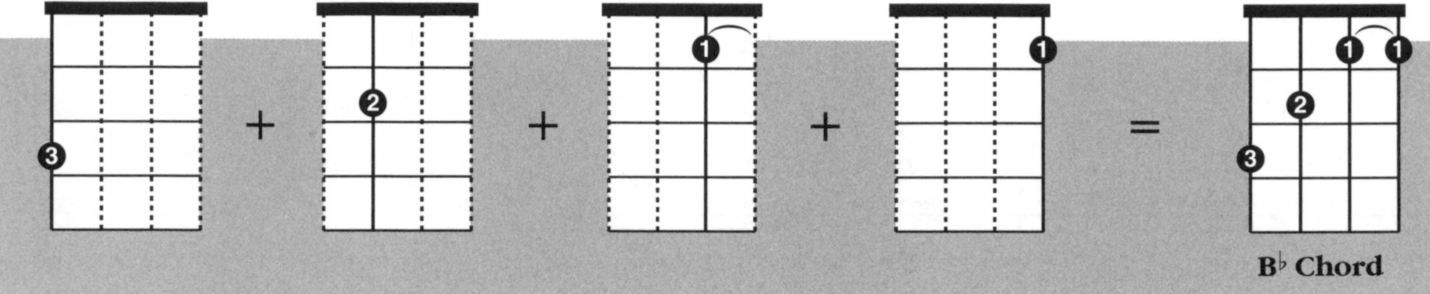

How to Play the F7 Chord

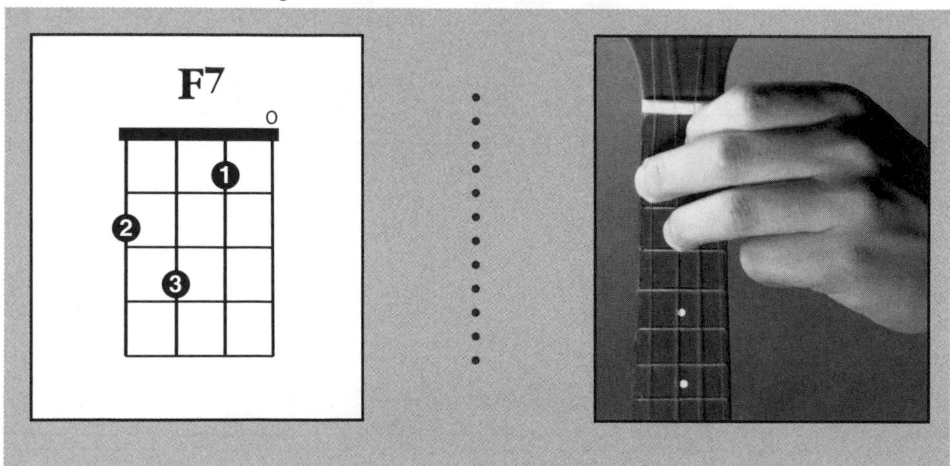

Place ❶, ❷ and ❸ in position, then play one string at a time:

Play all four strings together:

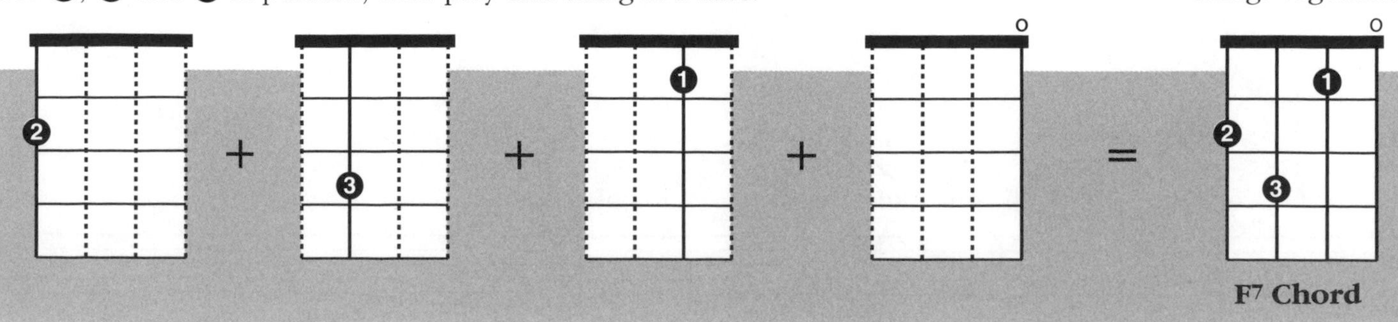

Play the following exercises until you can do them smoothly, without missing a beat. Then try the songs on the next few pages.

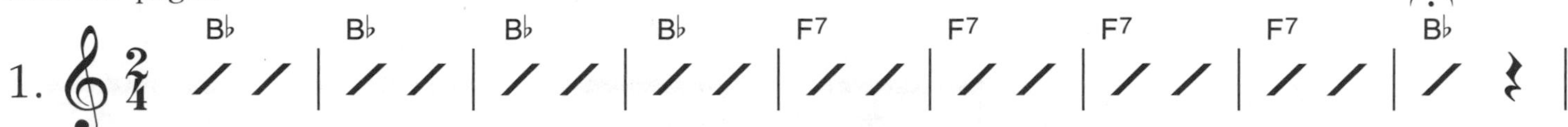

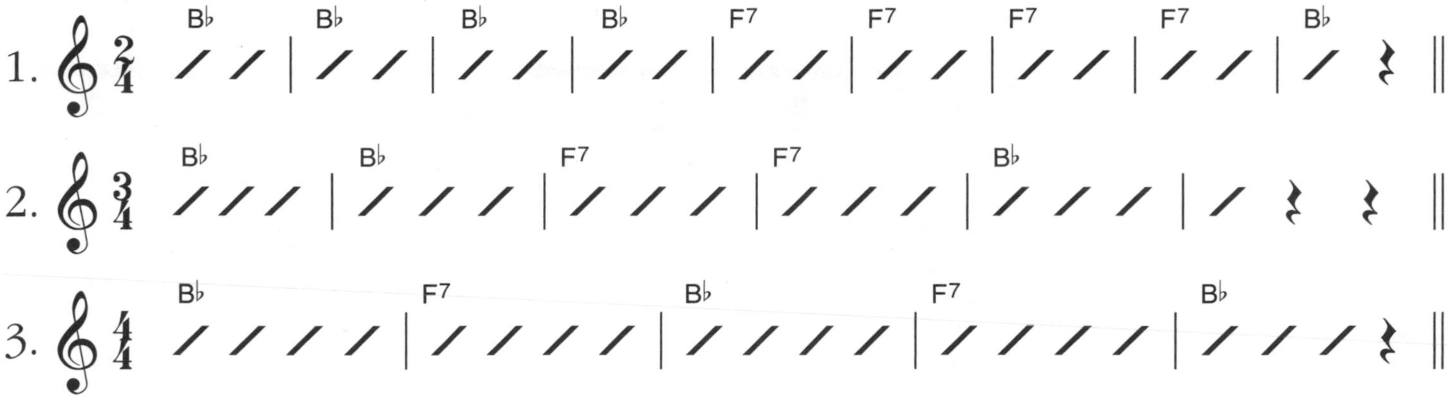

2. B♭ B♭ F7 F7 B♭

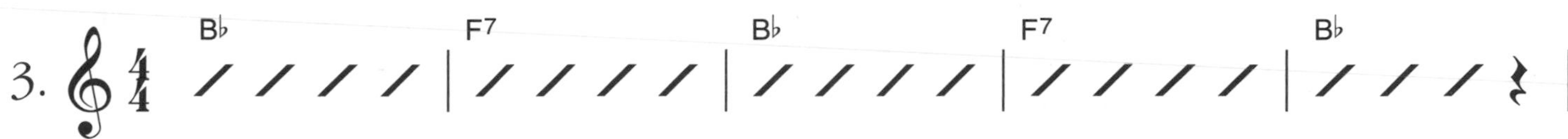

Skip to My Lou

American Square Dance Tune

The chords used in this song are:

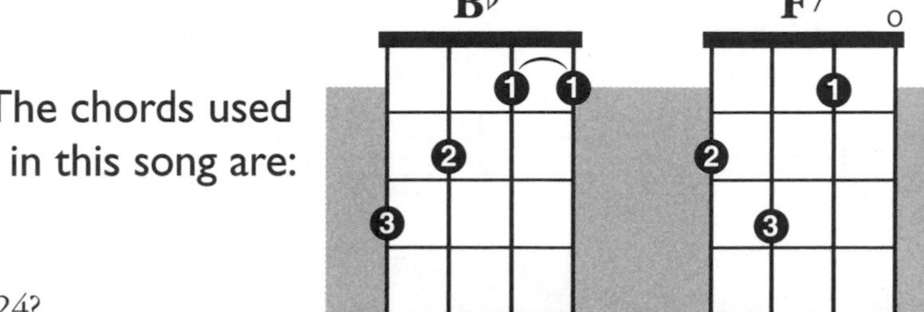

Remember the bluegrass strum you learned on page 24? It would sound good on this song also.

Moderately

B♭ Lost my part - ner, B♭ what-'ll I do? F7 Lost my part - ner, F7 what-'ll I do?

B♭ Lost my part - ner, B♭ what-'ll I do? F7 Skip to my Lou, my B♭ dar - ling.

B♭ Skip, skip, B♭ skip to my Lou, F7 Skip, skip, F7 skip to my Lou,

B♭ Skip, skip, B♭ skip to my Lou, F7 skip to my Lou, my B♭ dar - ling.

Verse 2:

B♭ Fly in the but - ter - milk, B♭ shoo, fly, shoo.

F7 Fly in the but - ter - milk, F7 shoo, fly, shoo.

B♭ Fly in the but - ter - milk, B♭ shoo, fly, shoo.

F7 Skip to my Lou, my B♭ dar - ling

Skip, skip etc.

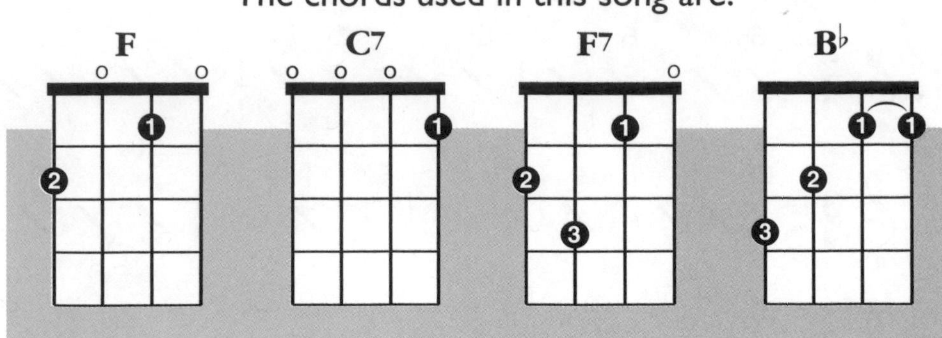

Red River Valley

American Cowboy Song

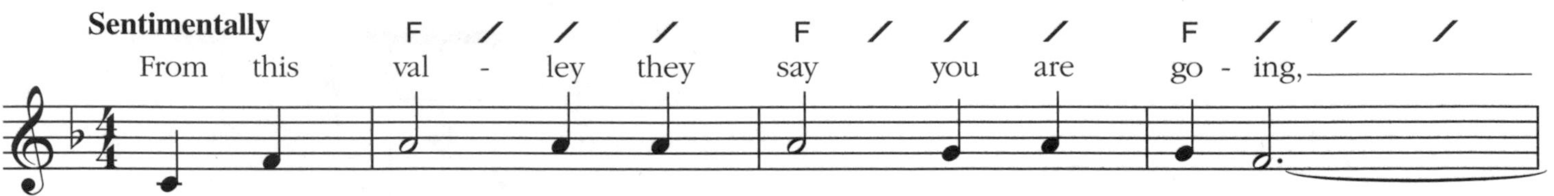

The chords used in this song are:

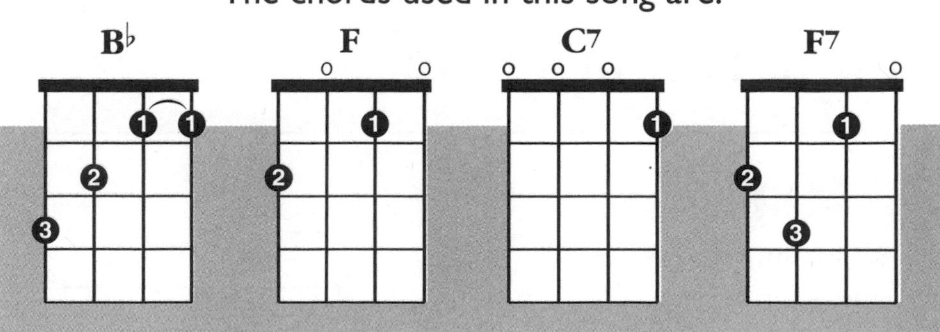

This Land Is Your Land

Words and Music by
Woody Guthrie

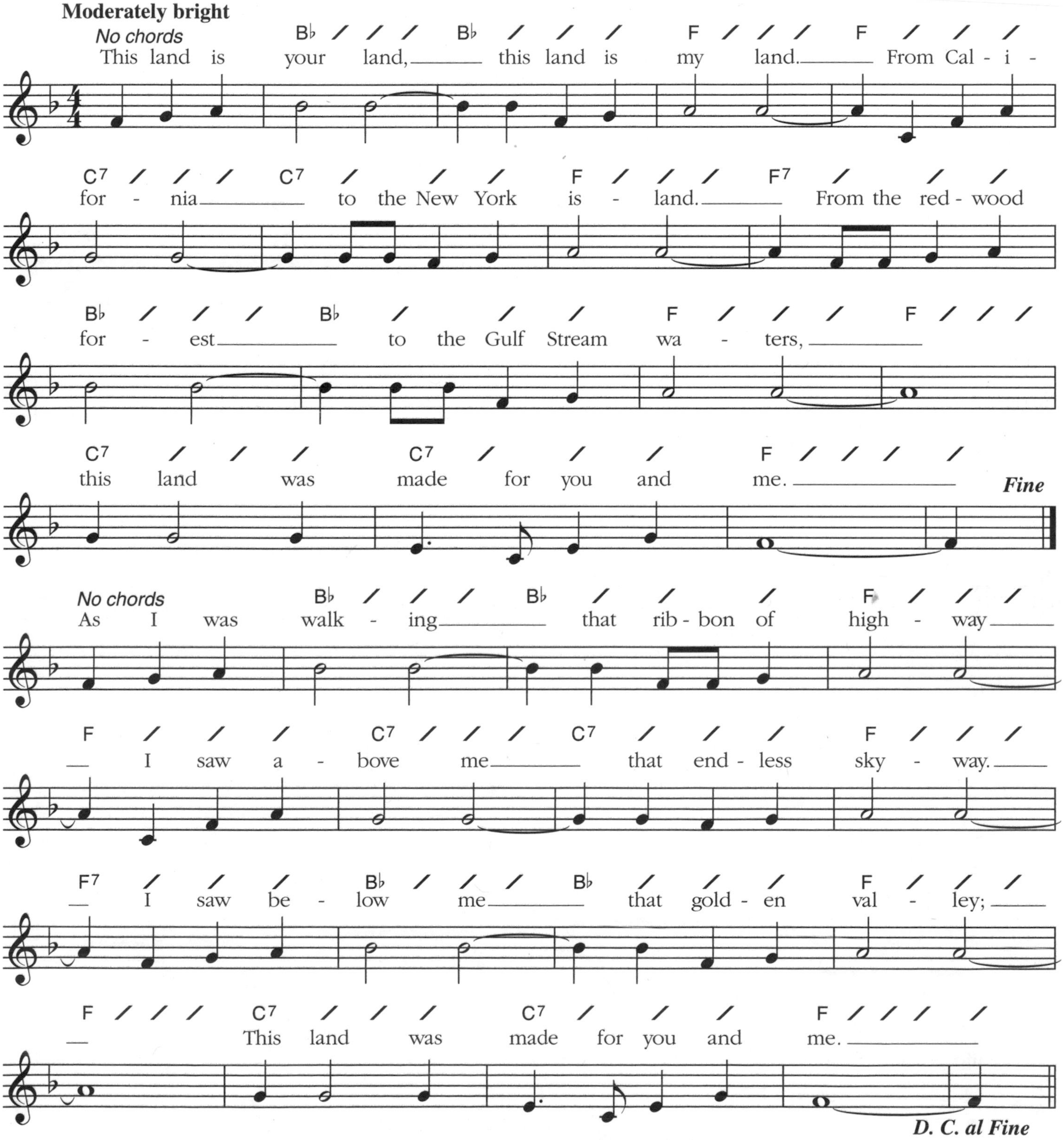

Moderately bright

No chords

B♭ / / / B♭ / / / F / / / F / / /
This land is your land, this land is my land. From Cal - i -

C7 / / / C7 / / / F / / / F7 / / /
for - nia to the New York is - land. From the red - wood

B♭ / / / B♭ / / / F / / / F / / /
for - est to the Gulf Stream wa - ters,

C7 / / / C7 / / / F / / / /
this land was made for you and me.

Fine

No chords

B♭ / / / B♭ / / / F / / /
As I was walk - ing that rib - bon of high - way

F / / / C7 / / / C7 / / / F / / /
I saw a - bove me that end - less sky - way.

F7 / / / B♭ / / / B♭ / / / F / / /
I saw be - low me that gold - en val - ley;

F / / / C7 / / / C7 / / / F / / / /
This land was made for you and me.

D. C. al Fine

How to Play in $\frac{6}{8}$ Time

Though $\frac{6}{8}$ time means there are 6 beats in each measure, it is usually accompanied as if it were $\frac{2}{4}$ time, or 2 beats per measure.

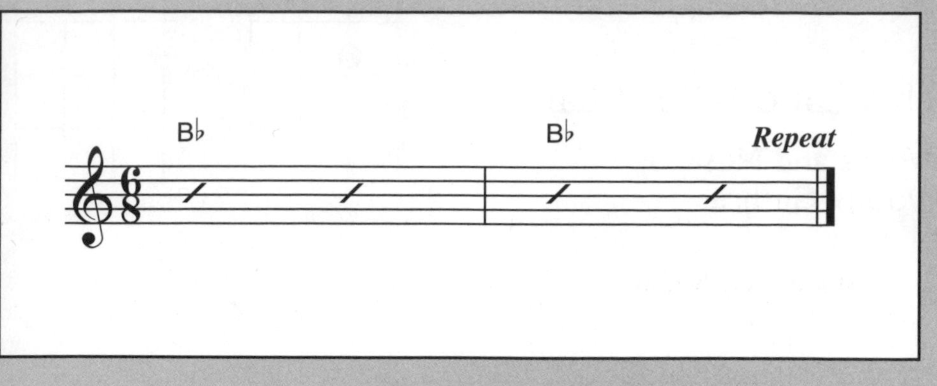

The chords used in this song are:

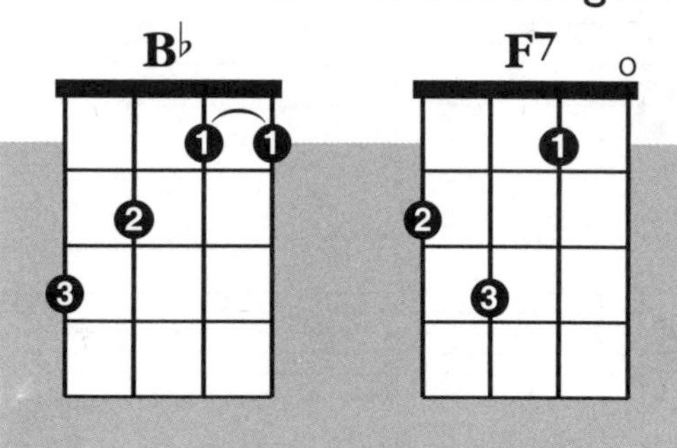

Row, Row, Row Your Boat

English Round

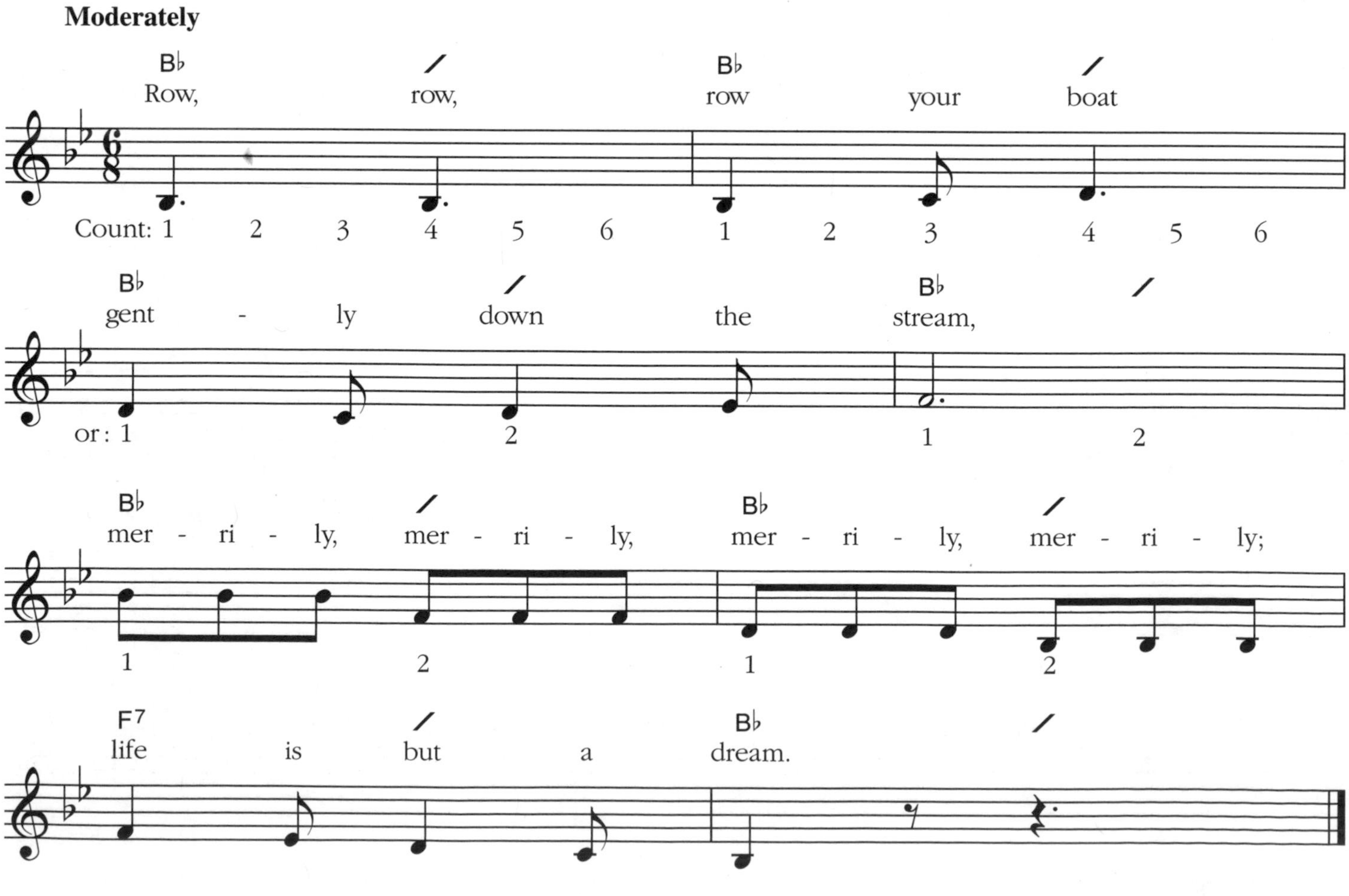

Moderately

B♭ / B♭ /
Row, row, row your boat

Count: 1 2 3 4 5 6 1 2 3 4 5 6

B♭ / B♭ /
gent - ly down the stream,

or: 1 2 1 2

B♭ / B♭ /
mer - ri - ly, mer - ri - ly, mer - ri - ly, mer - ri - ly;

1 2 1 2

F7 / B♭ /
life is but a dream.

The chords used in this song are:

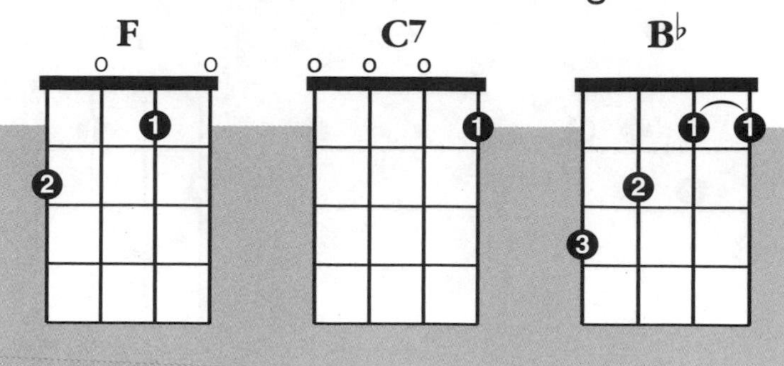

Vive L'Amour

English Drinking Song

Vive la compagnie is pronounced *vee*-vuh la *com*-pang-*ee* (more or less). It means "long live the company" (of soldiers).

Vive l'amour is pronounced *vee*-vuh la-*moore* and means "long live love."

Brightly

F / F / F C7
Let ev - 'ry good fel - low now fill up his glass, Vi - ve la com - pa -

F / F / F /
gnie! And drink to the health of his beau - ti - ful lass,

F C7 F / F /
Vi - ve la com - pa - gnie! Vi - ve la, vi - ve la,

B♭ / C7 / F /
vi - ve l'a - mour, Vi - ve la, vi - ve la, vi - ve l'a - mour,

F / B♭ / C7 / F /
Vi - ve la, vi - ve la, vi - ve l'a-mour, Vi - ve la com - pa - gnie!

The chords used in this song are:

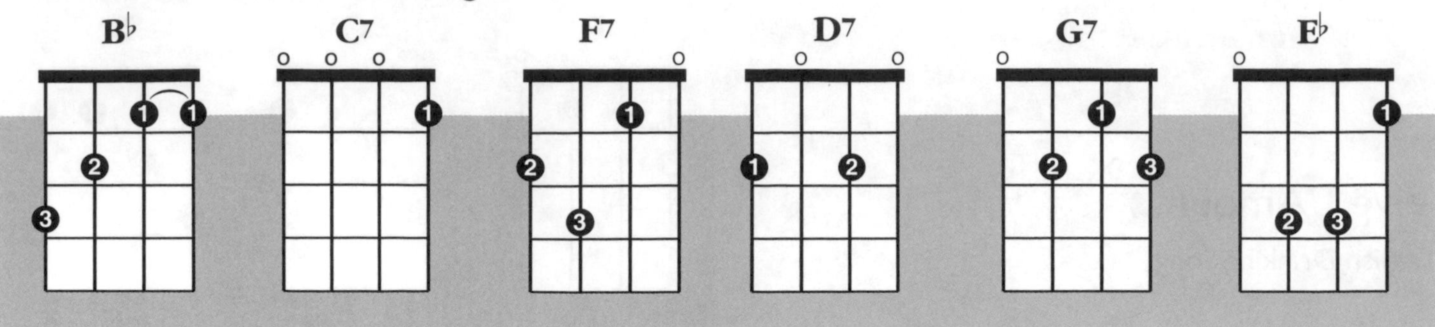

Notice the new chord: E♭. As you have with all the other chords, learn it one finger at a time.

Aura Lee

Civil War Song

Moderately slow

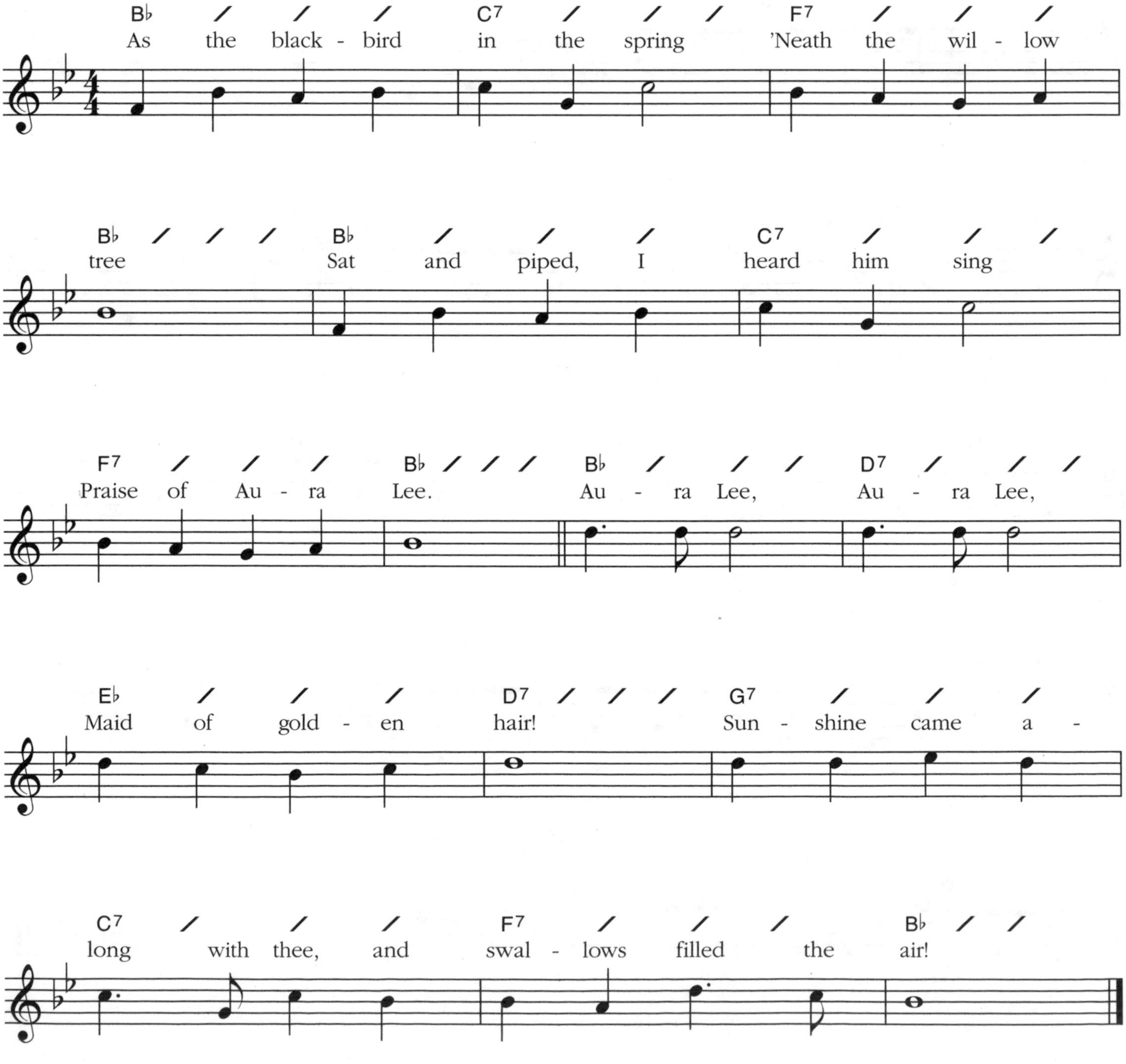

B♭ / / / C7 / / / F7 / / /
As the black - bird in the spring 'Neath the wil - low

B♭ / / / B♭ / / / C7 / / /
tree Sat and piped, I heard him sing

F7 / / / B♭ / / / B♭ / / / D7 / / /
Praise of Au - ra Lee. Au - ra Lee, Au - ra Lee,

E♭ / / / D7 / / / G7 / / /
Maid of gold - en hair! Sun - shine came a -

MINI MUSIC LESSON

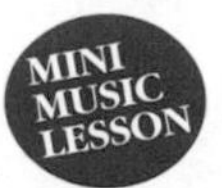

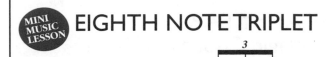

EIGHTH NOTE TRIPLET

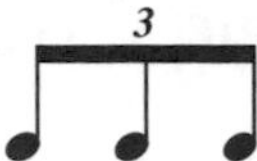

This musical figure is called an eighth note triplet.
It means that the three eighth notes are played in one beat.

The chords used in this song are:

B♭
F
C
C7

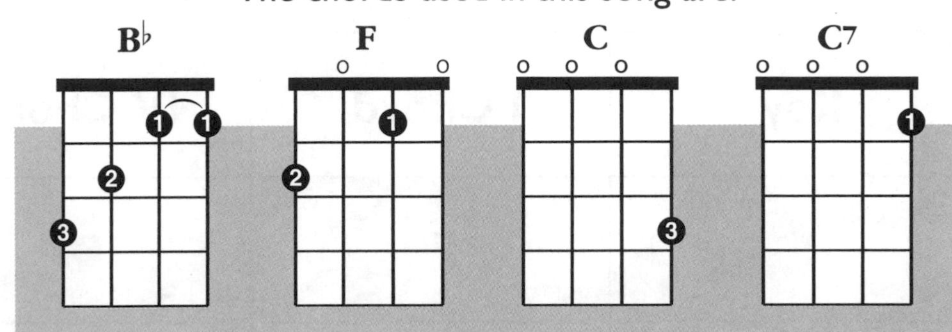

Amazing Grace

Words by John Newton
Music: Traditional

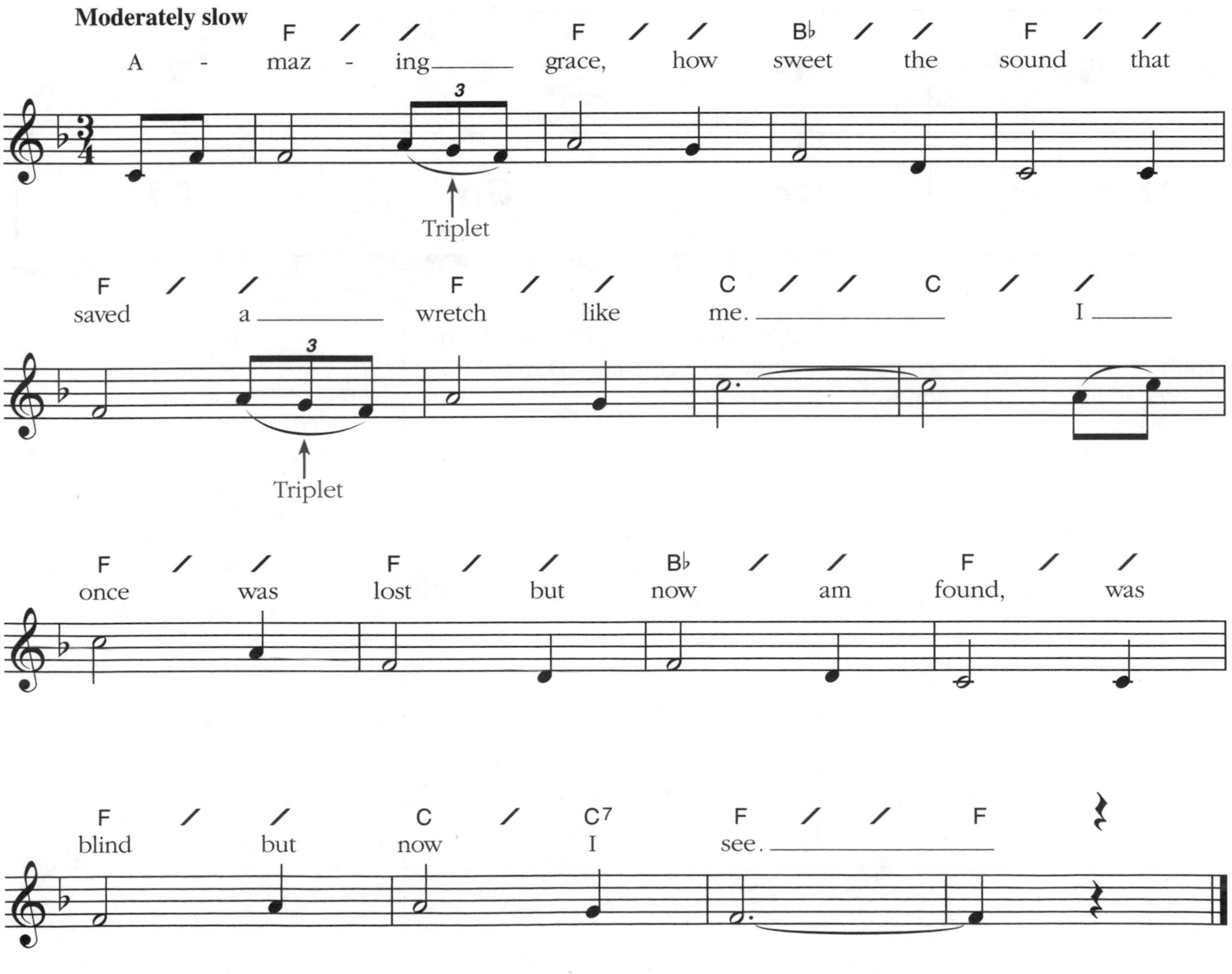

Moderately slow
F / / F / / B♭ / / F / /
A - maz - ing grace, how sweet the sound that
3
Triplet
F / / F / / C / / C / /
saved a wretch like me. I
3
Triplet
F / / F / / B♭ / / F / /
once was lost but now am found, was
F / / C / C7 F / / F
blind but now I see.

MINI MUSIC LESSON

HOW TO PLAY BY EAR
Using Three Magic Chords

There are thousands of folk songs, country songs, early rock 'n' roll songs and blues songs that can be played using only three simple chords. Musicians call these the I (one), IV (four) and V7 (five-seven) chords. You already know all of these chords:

Key	I Chord	IV Chord	V7 Chord
F	F	B♭	C7
C	C	F	G7
G	G	C	D7
D minor	Dm	Gm	A7

As you can see, each key has a family of three chords which can be used to accompany many songs in that key.

You can review all of these chords in the Ukulele Chord Dictionary on pages 58–64.

HOW TO DETERMINE THE KEY OF A SONG

Any song can be played in any key, but you'll find that it is easier for your voice if you choose the best key. Since everyone's voice is different, don't expect that your key will necessarily work for someone else.

Try this: Start strumming an F chord. Once you have the sound of it in your ear, begin singing "Oh Susanna!" If you're a male with an average voice or a female soprano, this key will probably be comfortable for you. You can then say "I sing 'Oh, Susanna!' in the key of F." If this key is too high or too low, try the next key on the list, the key of C. If neither key works, try the next key on the list. Find the key that doesn't strain your voice. (Since only a few songs are in a minor key, you may ignore the key of D minor for now.)

HOW TO PLAY AN ENTIRE SONG BY EAR

Once you've determined the key of the song, review the three magic chords you'll use. Let's say you're going to sing "Oh, Susanna!" in the key of F. The three magic chords are F, B♭ and C7.

Strum the I chord, F, and start singing until it seems a new chord is called for.

F / / / / / / / / / / / /
Oh, I come from Al - a - bam - a with a ban - jo on my . . .

You can hear that on the word "knee" a new chord must be played. Try the IV chord in the key of F, the B♭ chord. Nope, that doesn't sound right. . . try the V7 chord. Yes, that does sound right:

C7 / / /
Knee, and I'm . . .

On the word "goin'" we need another new chord. The IV, or B♭? No. How about going back to the I (the F)? Yes, that sounds right.

F / / / / / / / / / C7 / F / / /
goin' to Lou' - si - an - na for my true love (new chord) for to (new chord) see.

Now we get to use the IV chord or B♭.

B♭ / / / / / / / F / / / C7 / /
Oh, Su - san - na oh (new chord) don't you cry for (new chord) me.

See if you can work out the rest of it yourself.

Things to Remember

When working out a song by ear, keep these three major points in mind:

1. Most songs are in major keys. You know three possible major keys now: F, C and G. Try these first.
2. Folk songs and other simple songs almost always begin on the I chord. That is, a song in the key of F almost always begins on a F chord. A song in the key of C begins on a C chord, and so on.
3. Songs always end on the I chord.

MINI MUSIC LESSON

HOW TO TRANSPOSE

Taking a song written in one key and playing it in another is called transposing. There are two important reasons why you might want to transpose a song.

1. It's written in a key that you don't know. If you buy collections of songs, you'll find that many of them will be in unfamiliar keys. To determine the key of a written song, look at the last chord in the song. If the last chord in the song is a G chord, the song is written in the key of G. That's fine, because you know the key of G. But what if the song is in B♭, or E♭ or A♭ or some other key that you don't know. What you do is transpose it to a key that you do know.
2. The song may be too high or too low for you to sing comfortably. Transposing the song into a more comfortable key will solve this problem.

The following chart will allow you to transpose from any key to any other key. Your main objective is to wind up in one of the three keys you know: F, C or G.

1	2	3	4	5	6
C	C♯/D♭	D	E♭	E	F
C♯/D♭	D	E♭	E	F	F♯/G♭
D	E♭	E	F	F♯/G♭	G
E♭	E	F	F♯/G♭	G	A♭
E	F	F♯/G♭	G	A♭	A
F	F♯/G♭	G	A♭	A	B♭
F♯/G♭	G	A♭	A	B♭	B
G	A♭	A	B♭	B	C
A♭	A	B♭	B	C	C♯/D♭
A	B♭	B	C	C♯/D♭	D
B♭	B	C	C♯/D♭	D	E♭
B	C	C♯/D♭	D	E♭	E

How to Use the Chart

1. Find the key the song is written in column 1. Let's say the song is in the unfamiliar key of D♭. Find D♭ in column 1.
2. Find the key you want to wind up in also in column 1. Let's say the key of G. You'll notice that G is six lines below D♭ in column 1.
3. Find the chords of the song in the D♭ row. Then replace them with the chords in the same column of the G row, exactly six lines below. For example, an G♭ chord would become a C chord. An A♭7 chord would become a D7 chord, and so on.

The chart can be used in this way to transpose from any key to any other key.

7	8	9	10	11	12
F♯/G♭	G	A♭	A	B♭	B
G	A♭	A	B♭	B	C
A♭	A	B♭	B	C	C♯/D♭
A	B♭	B	C	C♯/D♭	D
B♭	B	C	C♯/D♭	D	E♭
B	C	C♯/D♭	D	E♭	E
C	C♯D♭	D	E♭	E	F
C♯/D♭	D	E♭	E	F	F♯/G♭
D	E♭	E	F	F♯/G♭	G
E♭	E	F	F♯/G♭	G	A♭
E	F	F♯/G♭	G	A♭	A
F	F♯/G♭	G	A♭	A	B♭

UKULELE ACCOMPANIMENTS

Play these accompaniment patterns with either the index finger or a felt pick.

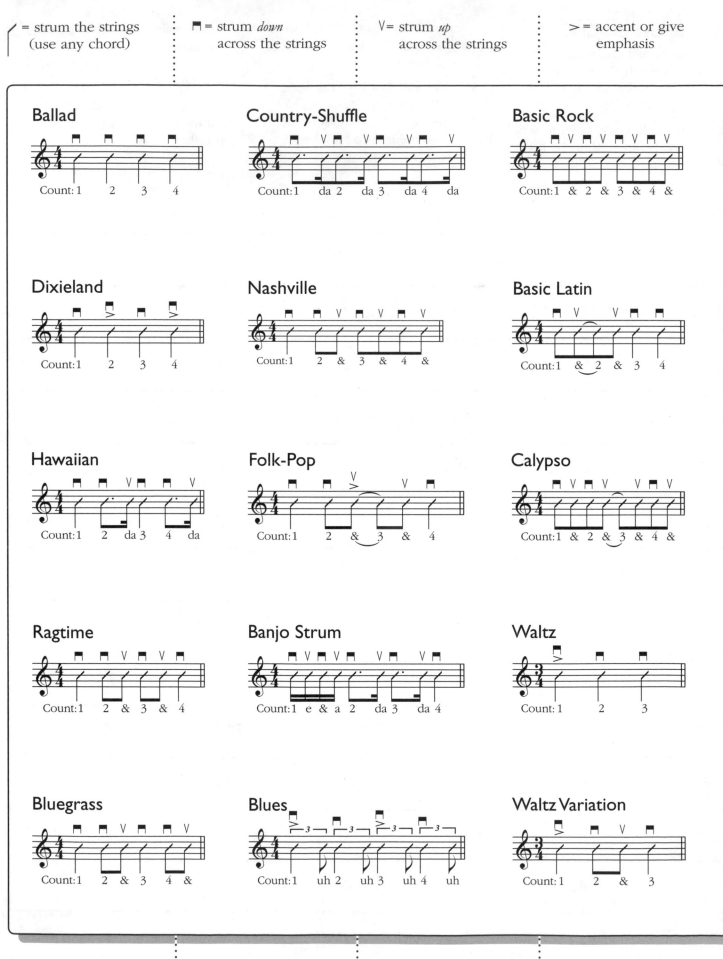

/ = strum the strings (use any chord)

⊓ = strum *down* across the strings

V = strum *up* across the strings

> = accent or give emphasis

Ballad

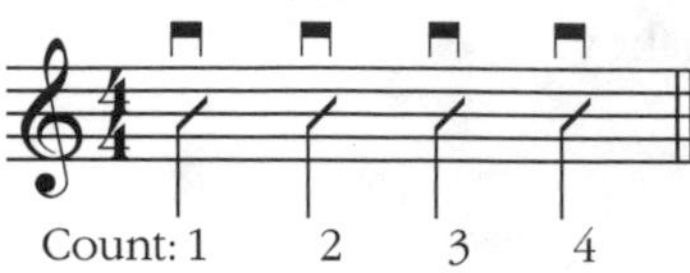

Country-Shuffle

Basic Rock

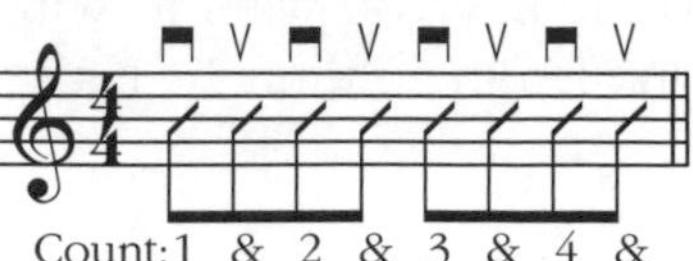

Dixieland

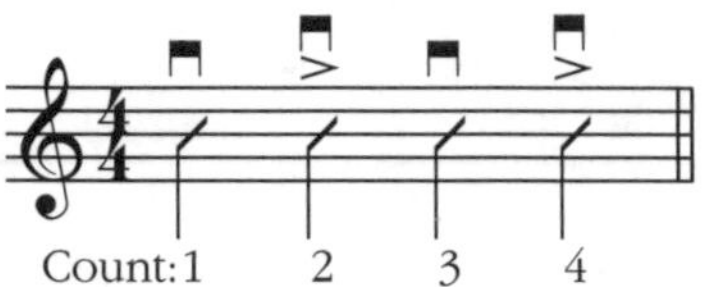

Nashville

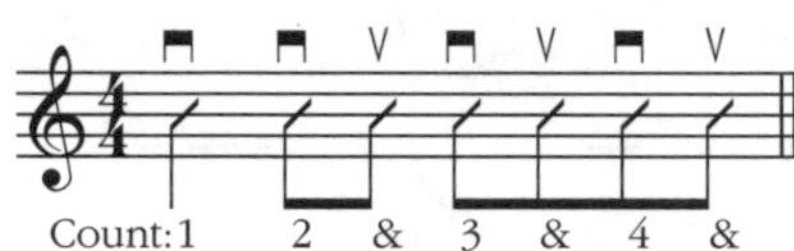

Basic Latin

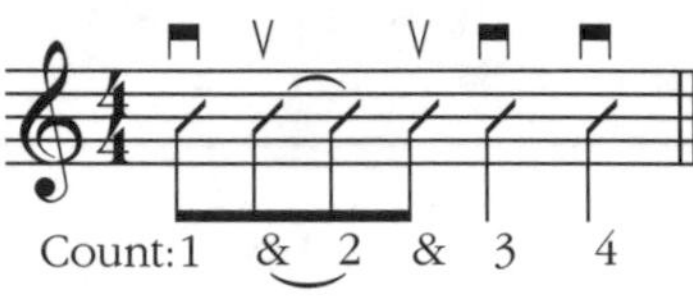

Hawaiian

Folk-Pop

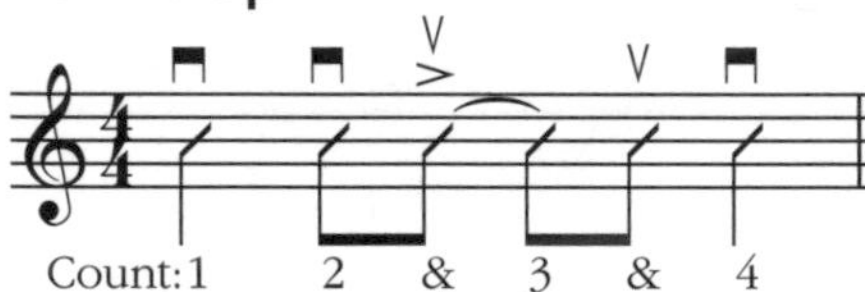

Calypso

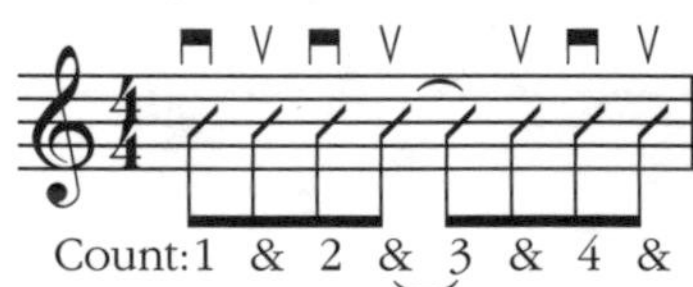

Ragtime

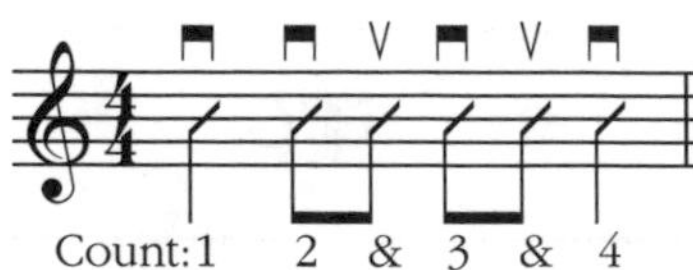

Banjo Strum

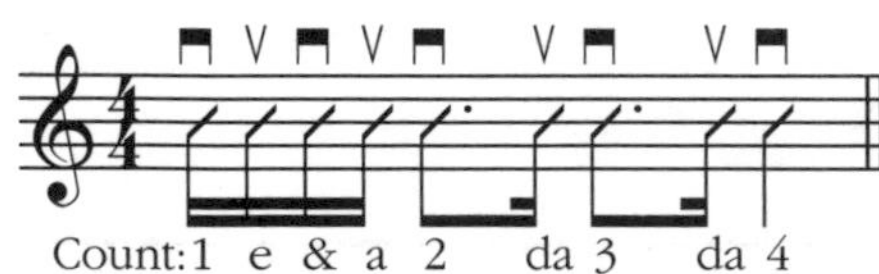

Waltz

Bluegrass

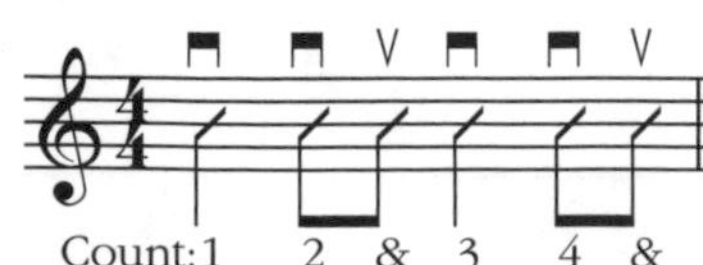

Blues

Waltz Variation

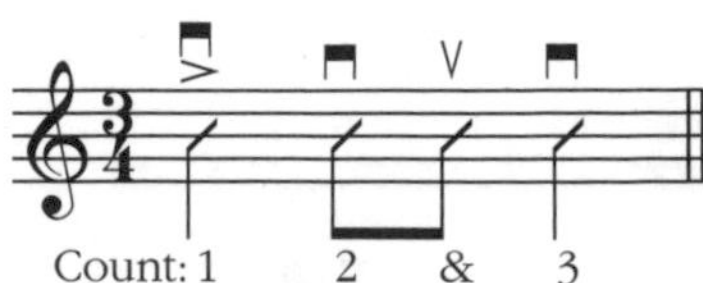

Ukulele Fingerboard Chart

Frets 1–12

STRINGS

FRETS	4th	3rd	2nd	1st
Open	G	C	E	A
1st Fret	G♯ A♭	C♯ D♭	F	A♯ B♭
2nd Fret	A	D	F♯/G♭	B
3rd Fret	A♯ B♭	D♯ E♭	G	C
4th Fret	B	E	G♯ A♭	C♯ D♭
5th Fret	C	F	A	D
6th Fret	C♯ D♭	F♯ G♭	A♯ B♭	D♯ E♭
7th Fret	D	G	B	E
8th Fret	D♯ E♭	G♯ A♭	C	F
9th Fret	E	A	C♯ D♭	F♯ G♭
10th Fret	F	A♯ B♭	D	G
11th Fret	F♯ G♭	B	D♯ E♭	G♯ A♭
12th Fret	G	C	E	A

Ukulele Chord Dictionary

On the following pages, we've compiled a dictionary of all the most commonly used chords. The letter (printed in a red box) is the name of the chord in G C E A tuning. If the key is too difficult, we've shown you how to transpose to an easier one.

The uke has always been a great instrument for parties and picnics, so have fun with it!

A

Major
A

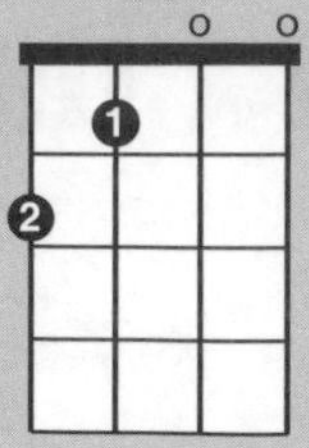

Minor
Am

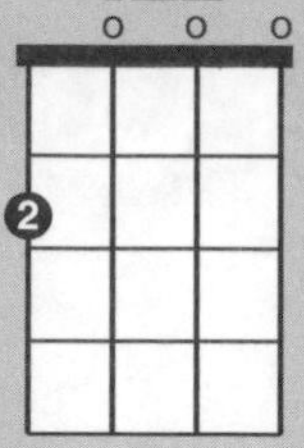

Seventh
A7

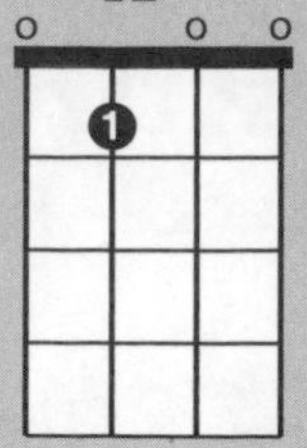

Major Sixth
A6
5th fret

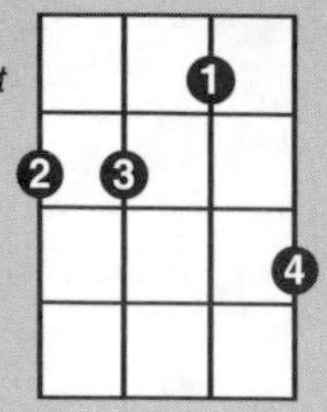

Minor Sixth
Am6
5th fret

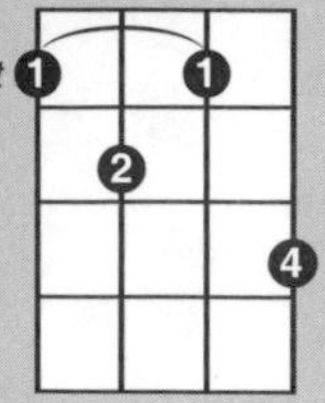

Major Seventh
Amaj7

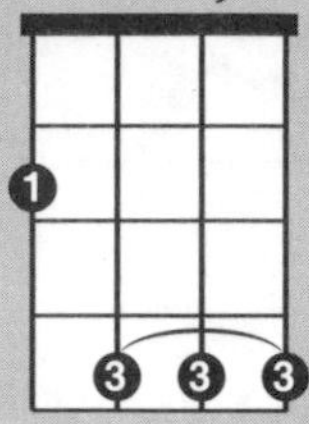

Minor Seventh
Am7

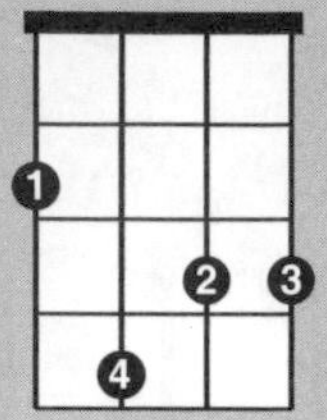

Augmented
A+

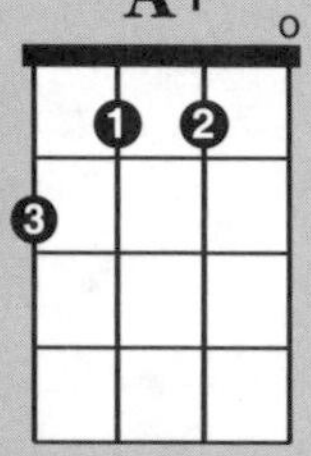

Diminished
A°

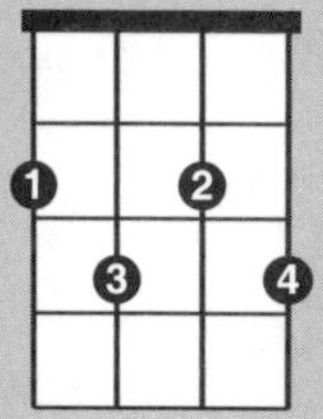

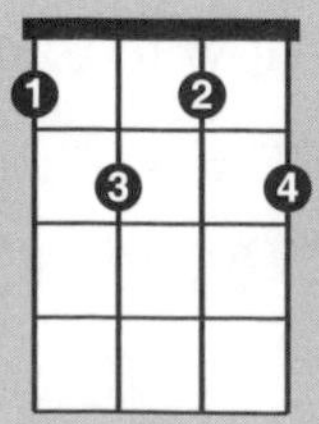

Dominant Ninth
A9

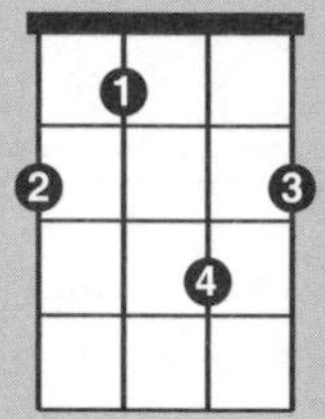

Dominant Thirteenth
A13
6th fret

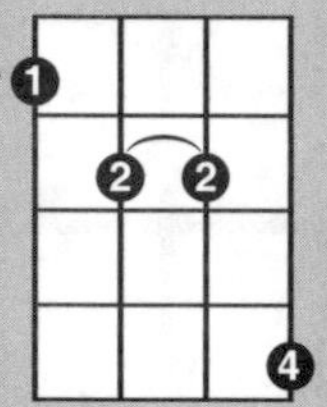

A♭

Same as G♯

Major
A♭
3rd fret

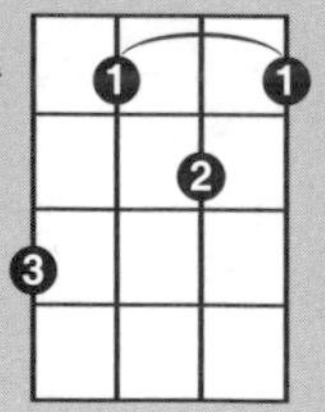

Minor
A♭m

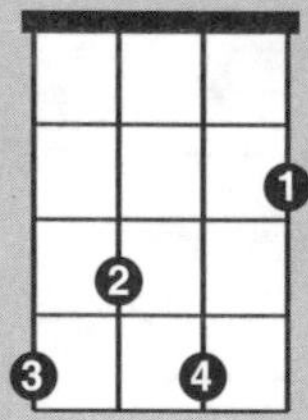

Seventh
A♭7

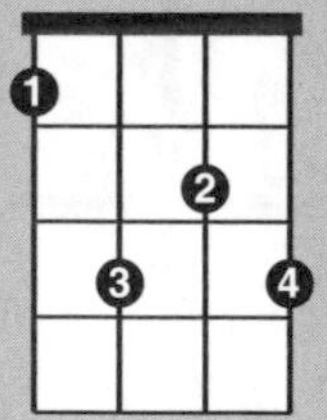

Major Sixth
A♭6
4th fret

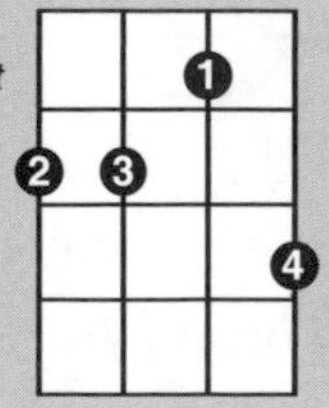

Minor Sixth
A♭m6
4th fret

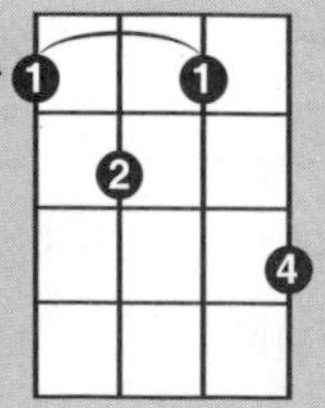

Major Seventh
A♭maj7

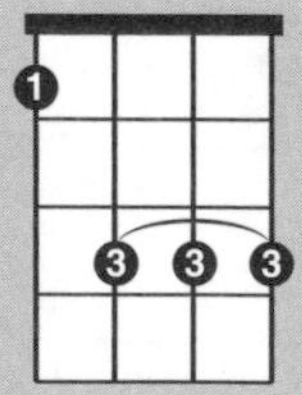

Minor Seventh
A♭m7

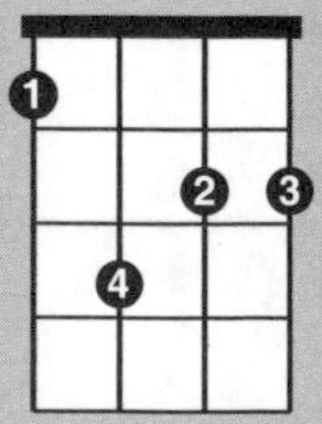

Augmented
A♭+

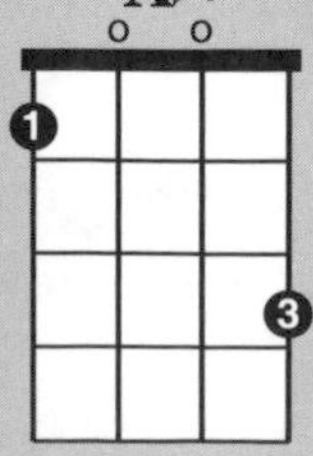

Diminished
A♭°

Dominant Ninth
A♭9
5th fret

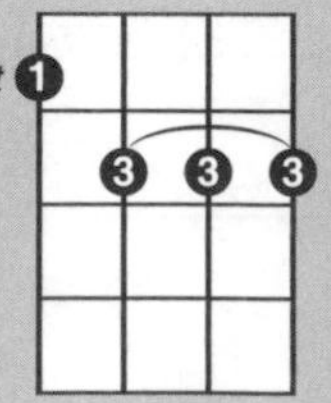

Dominant Thirteenth
A♭13
5th fret

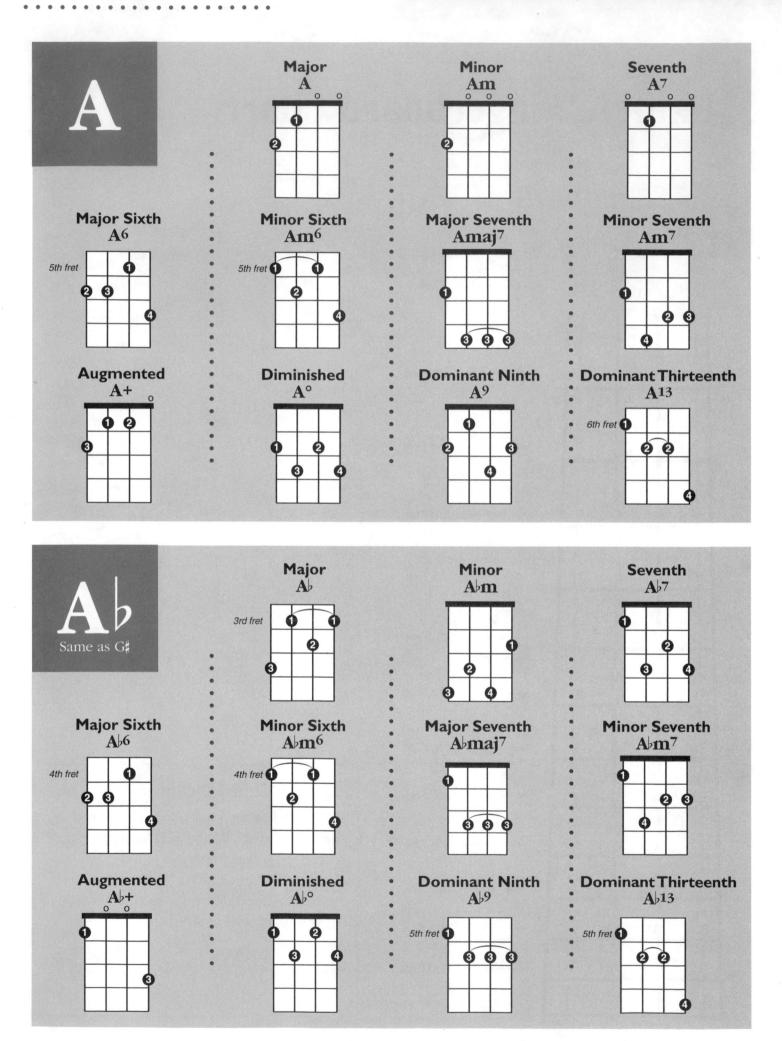

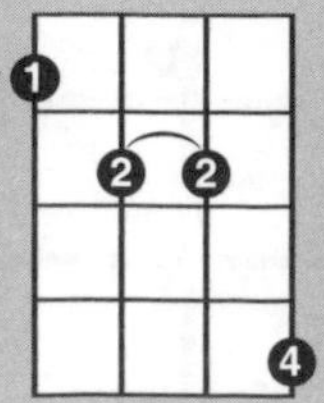

B

Same as C♭

Major
B

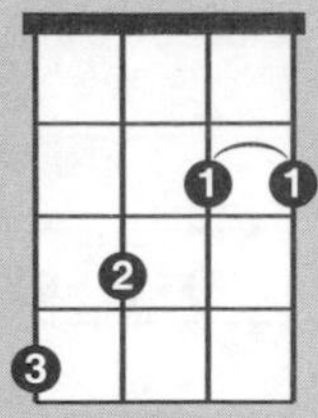

Minor
Bm

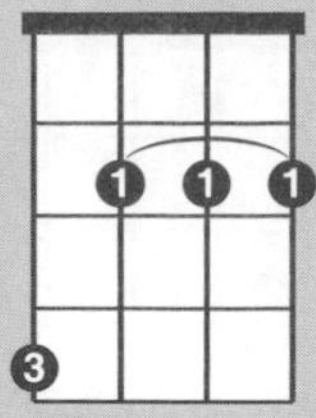

Seventh
B7

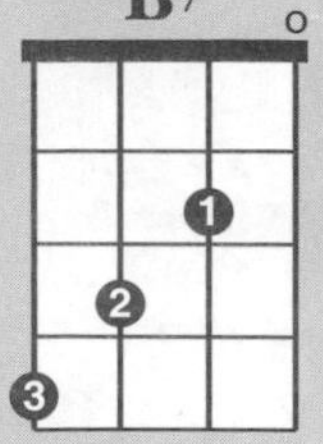

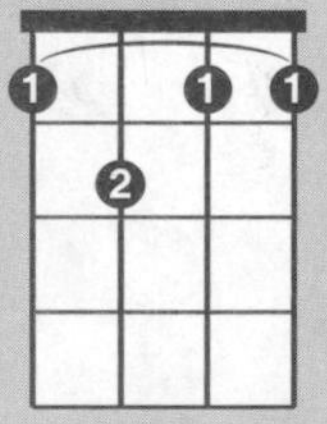

Major Sixth
B6

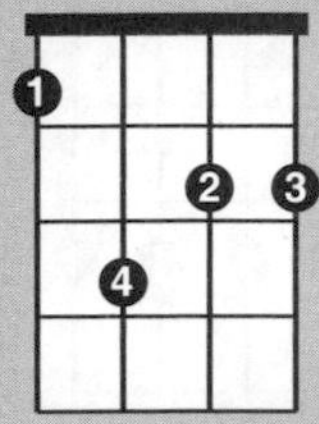

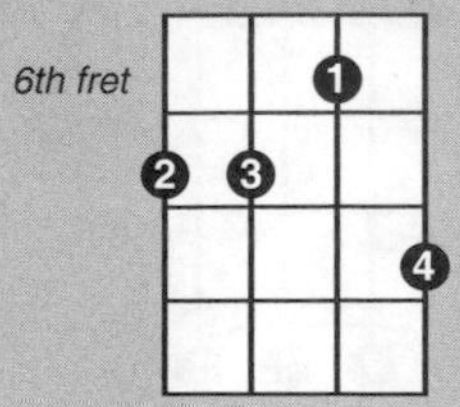

Minor Sixth
Bm6

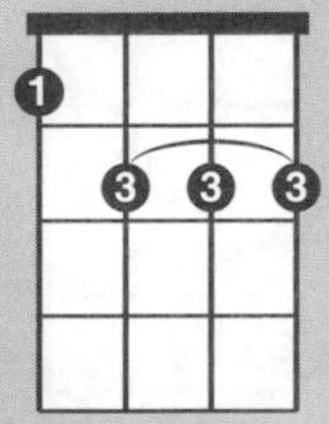

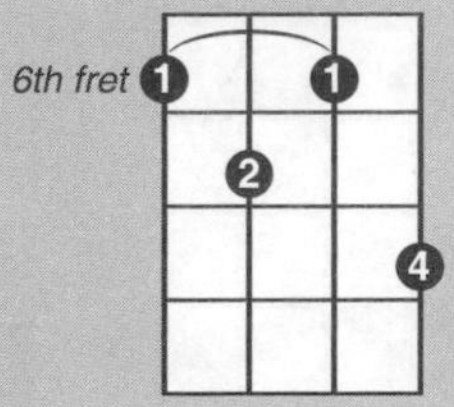

Major Seventh
Bmaj7

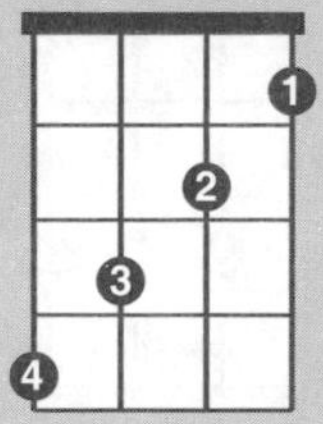

Minor Seventh
Bm7

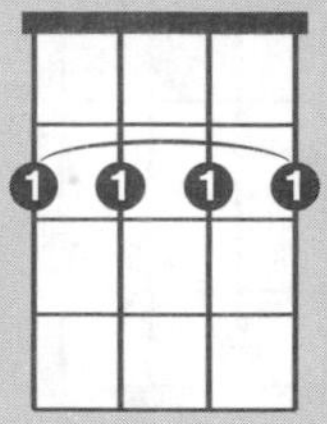

Augmented
B+

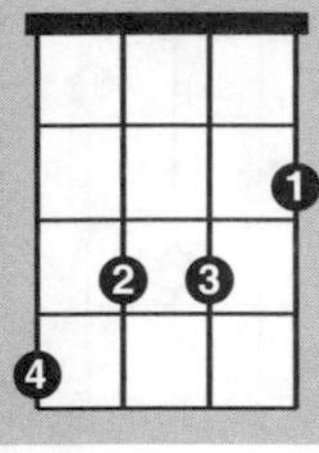

Diminished
B°

Dominant Ninth
B9

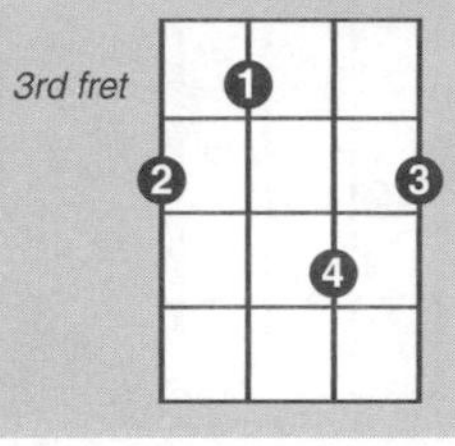

3rd fret

Dominant Thirteenth
B13

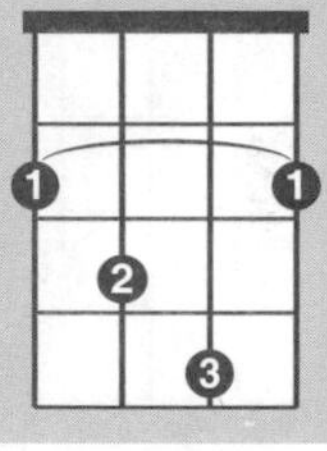

B♭

Major
B♭

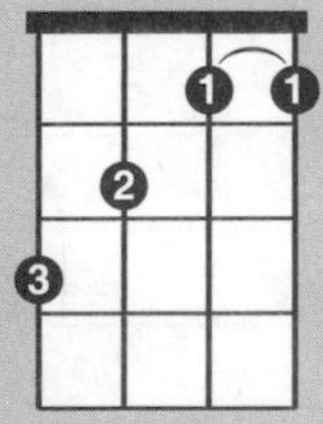

Minor
B♭m

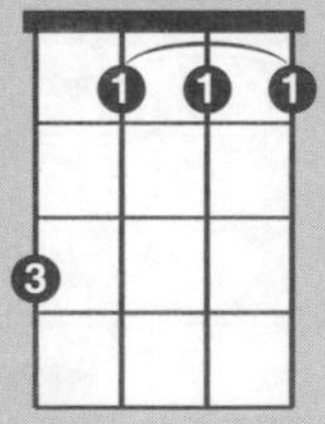

Seventh
B♭7

Major Sixth
B♭6

6th fret

Minor Sixth
B♭m6

6th fret

Major Seventh
B♭maj7

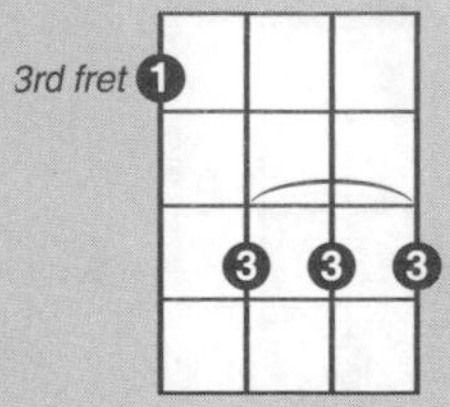

3rd fret

Minor Seventh
B♭m7

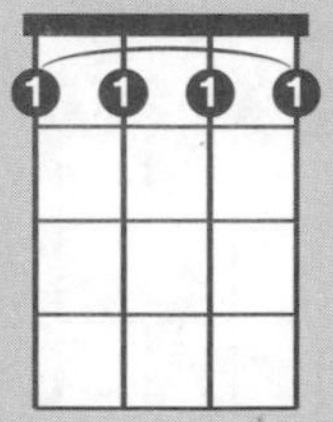

Augmented
B♭+

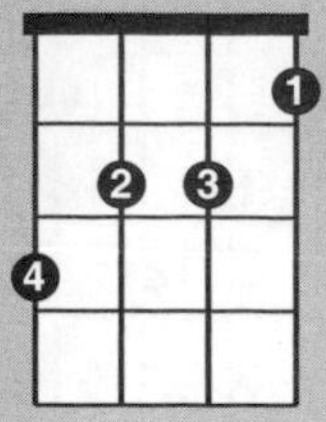

Diminished
B♭°

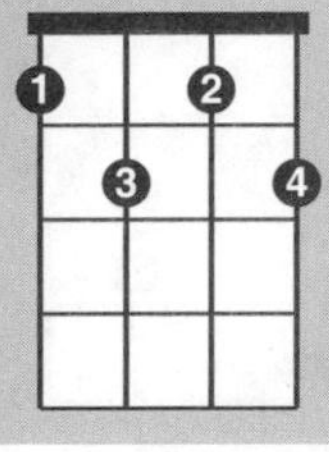

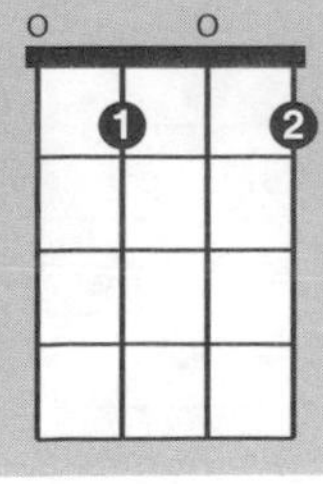

Dominant Ninth
B♭9

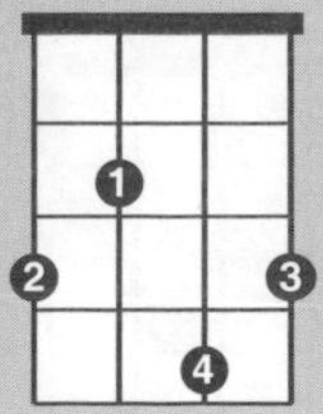

Dominant Thirteenth
B♭13

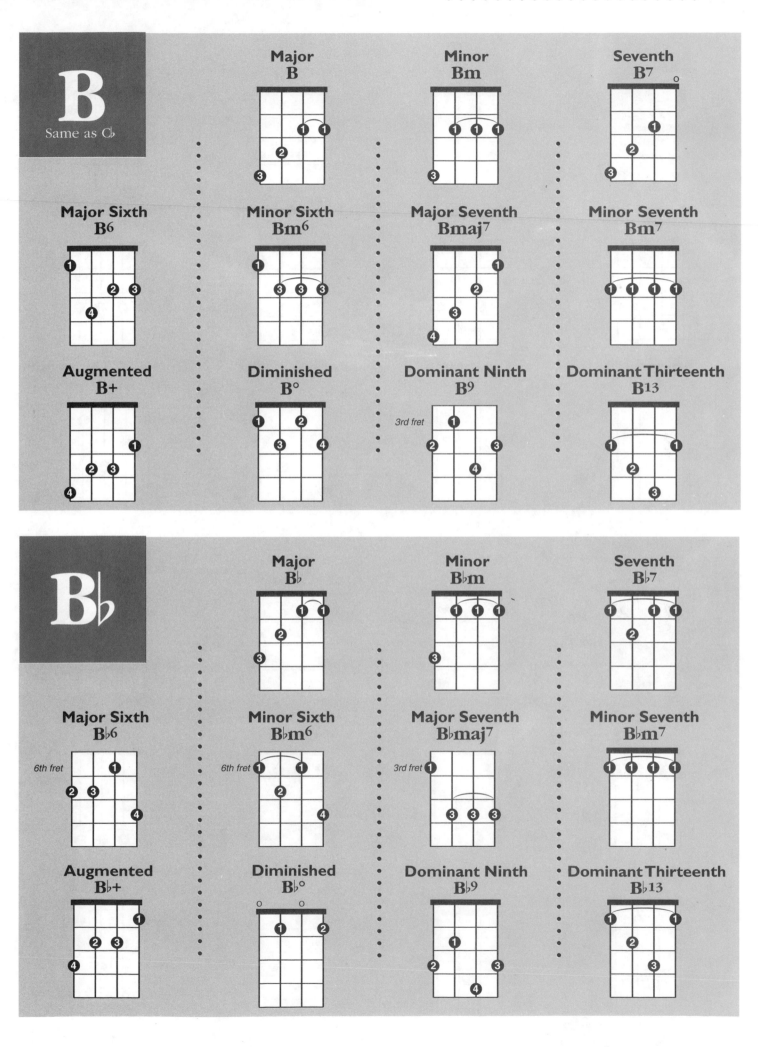

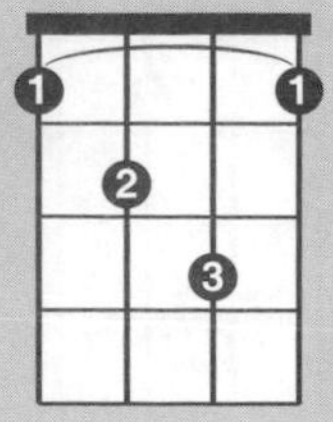

C

Major
C

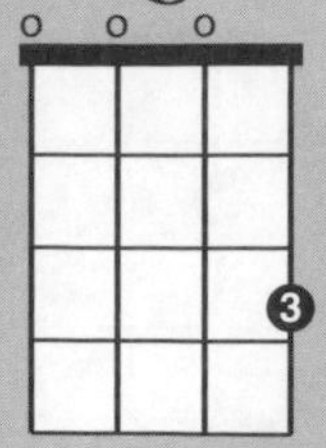

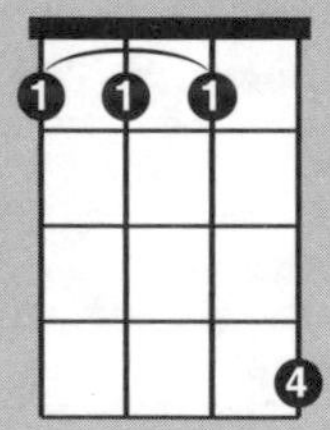

Minor
Cm

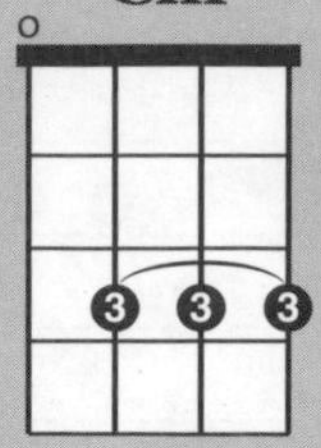

Seventh
C7

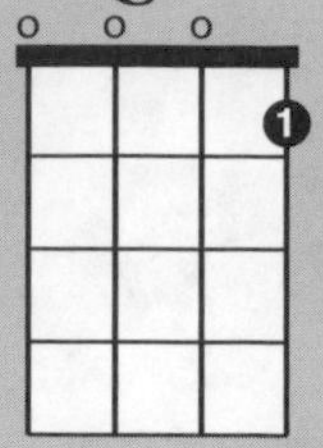

Major Sixth
C6

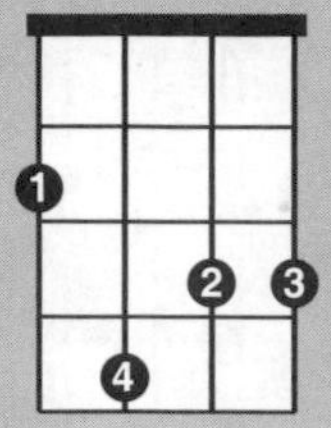

Minor Sixth
Cm6

Major Seventh
Cmaj7

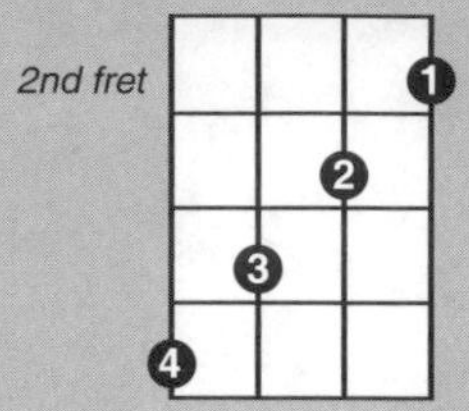

2nd fret

Minor Seventh
Cm7

Augmented
C+

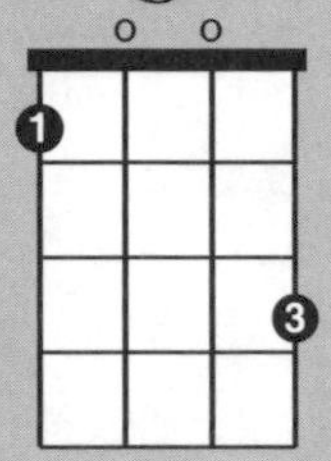

Diminished
C°

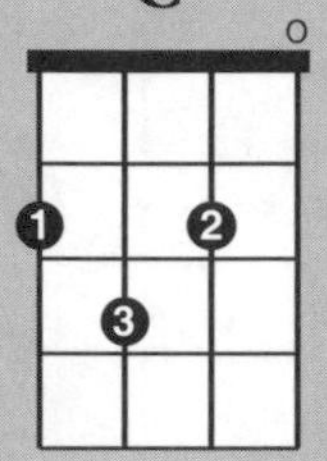

Dominant Ninth
C9

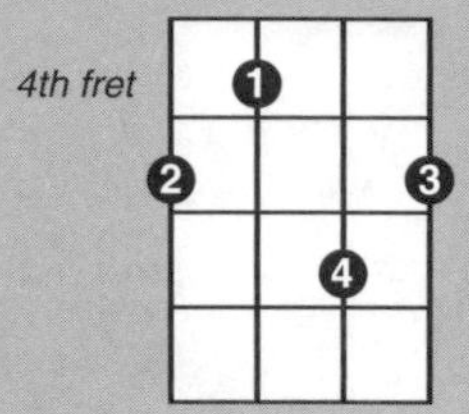

4th fret

Dominant Thirteenth
C13

3rd fret

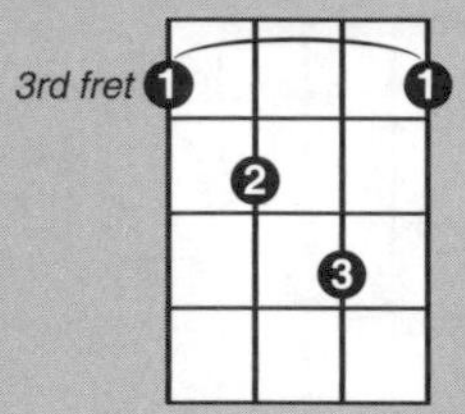

C♯

Same as D♭

Major
C♯

Minor
C♯m

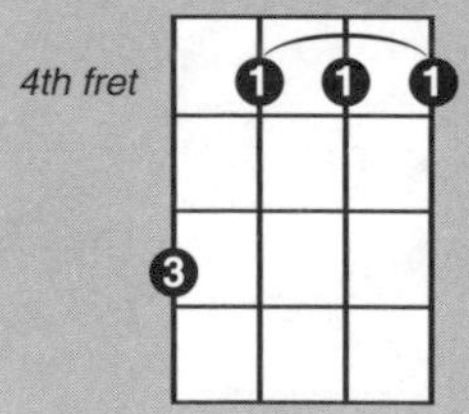

4th fret

Seventh
C♯7

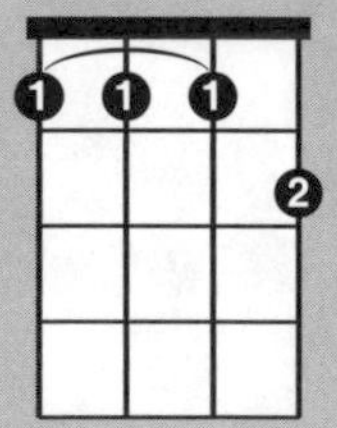

Major Sixth
C♯6

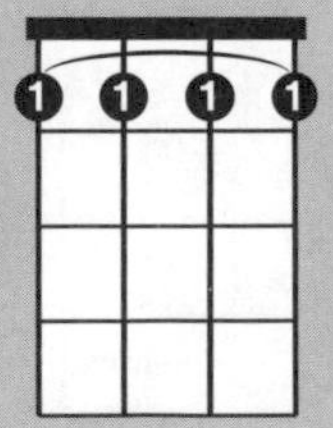

Minor Sixth
C♯m6

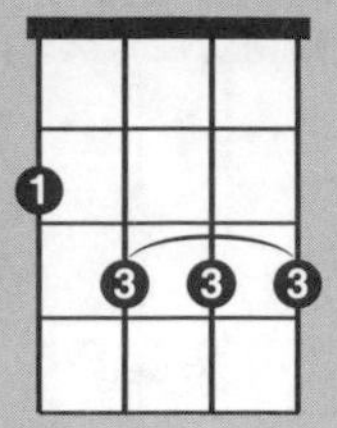

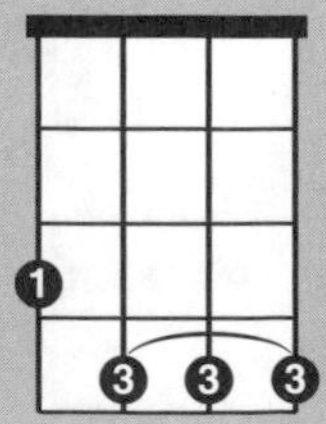

Major Seventh
C♯maj7

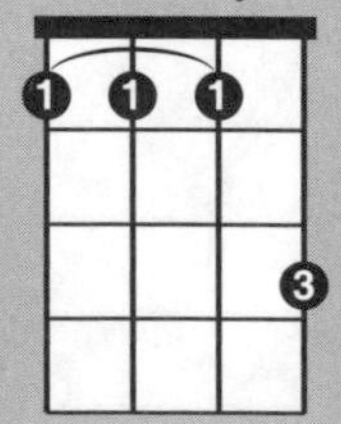

Minor Seventh
C♯m7

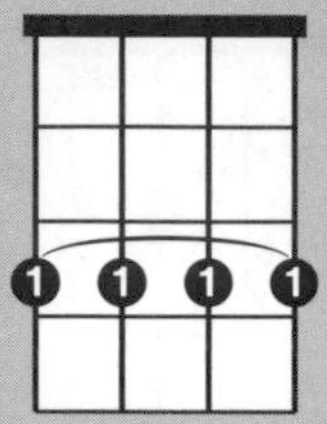

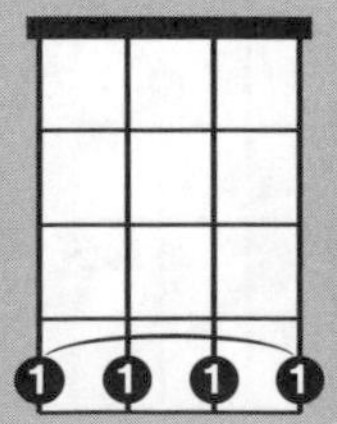

Augmented
C♯+

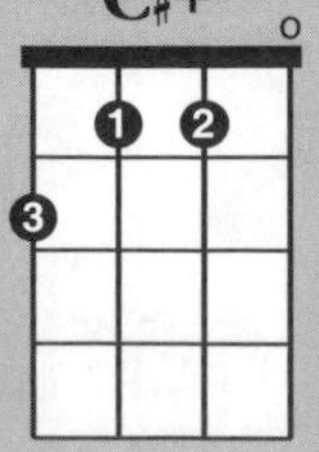

Diminished
C♯°

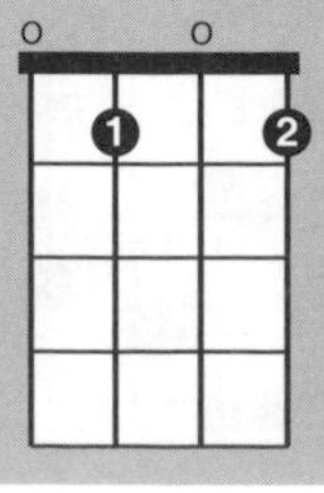

Dominant Ninth
C♯9

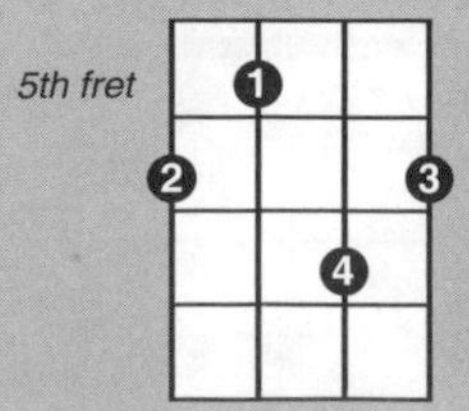

5th fret

Dominant Thirteenth
C♯13

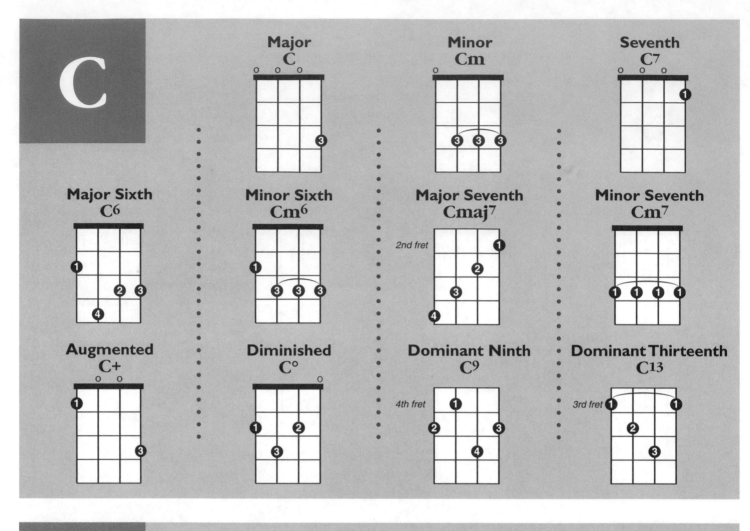

4th fret

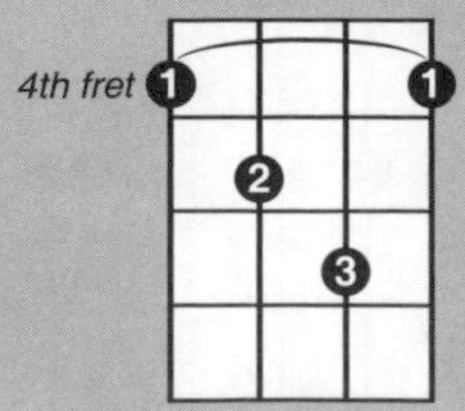

D

Major
D

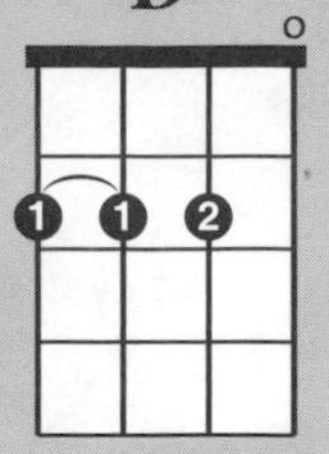

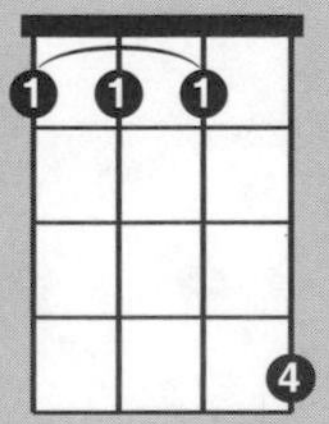

Minor
Dm

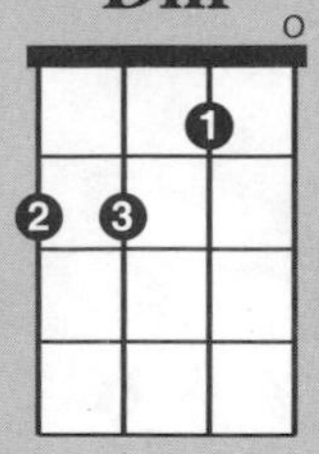

Seventh
D7

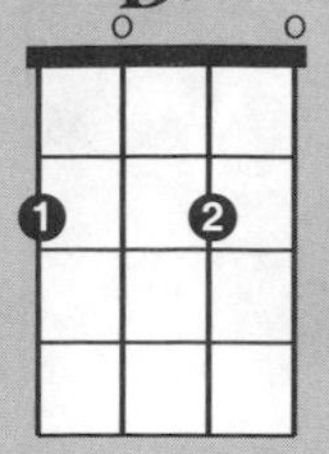

Major Sixth
D6

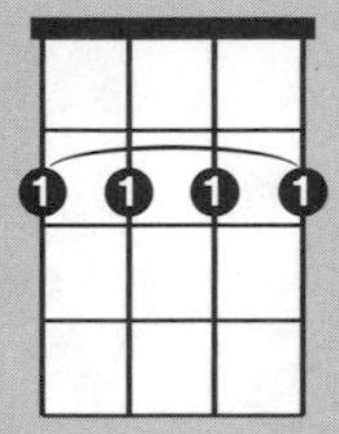

Minor Sixth
Dm6

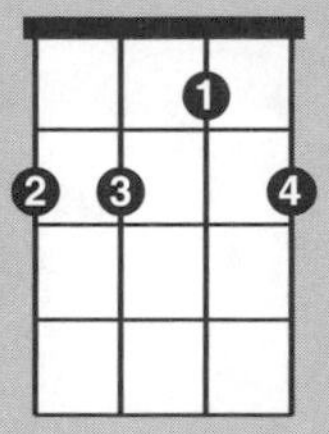

Major Seventh
Dmaj7

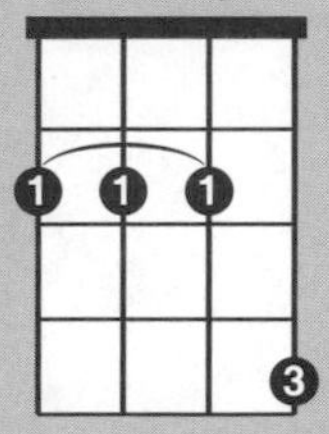

Minor Seventh
Dm7

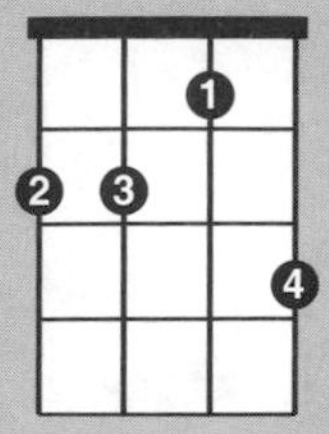

Augmented
D+

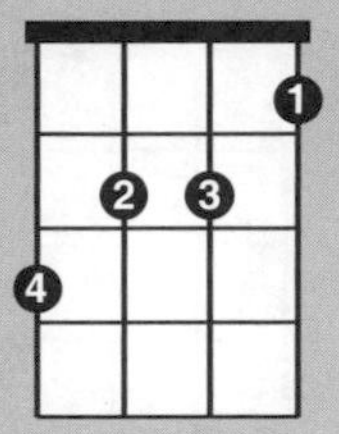

Diminished
D°

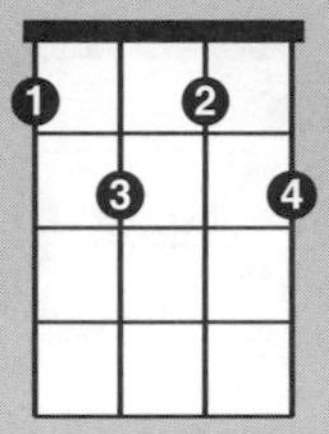

Dominant Ninth
D9

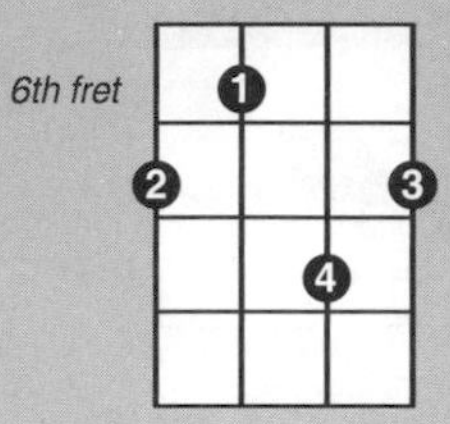

6th fret

Dominant Thirteenth
D13

5th fret

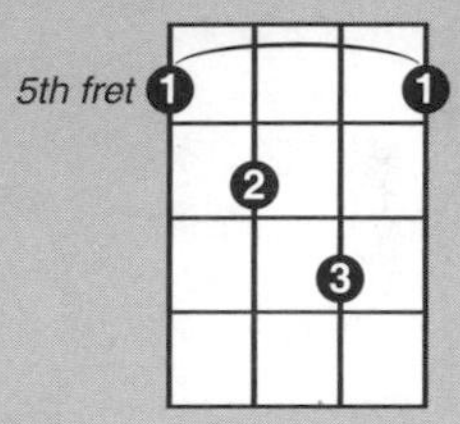

D♭

Same as C♯

Major
D♭

Minor
D♭m

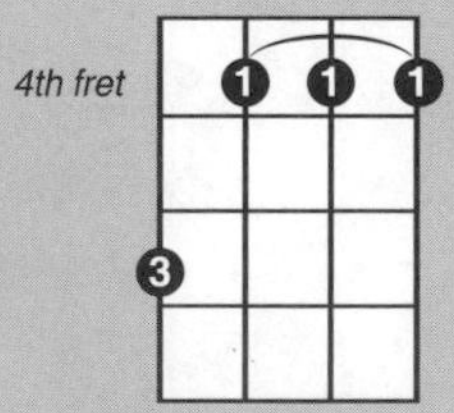

4th fret

Seventh
D♭7

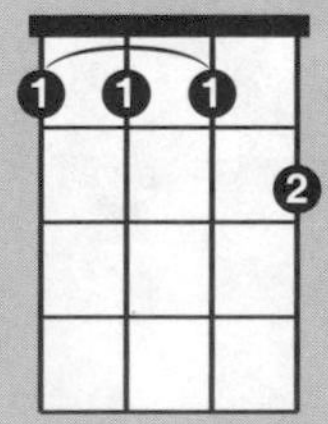

Major Sixth
D♭6

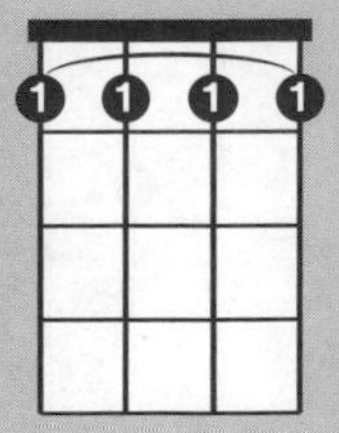

Minor Sixth
D♭m6

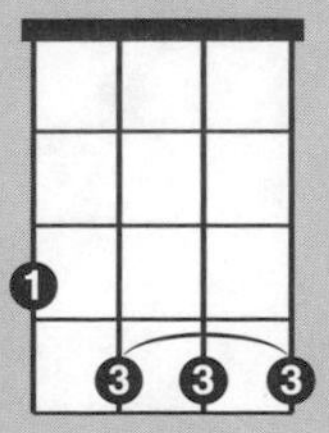

Major Seventh
D♭maj7

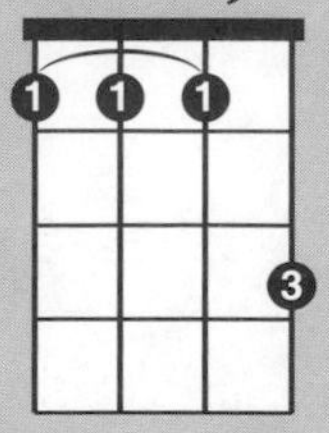

Minor Seventh
D♭m7

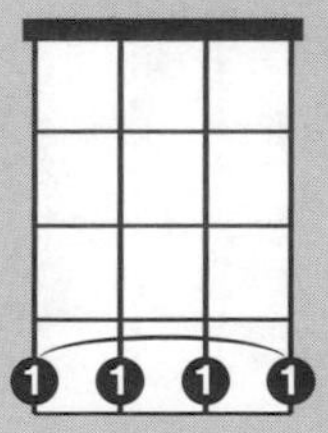

Augmented
D♭+

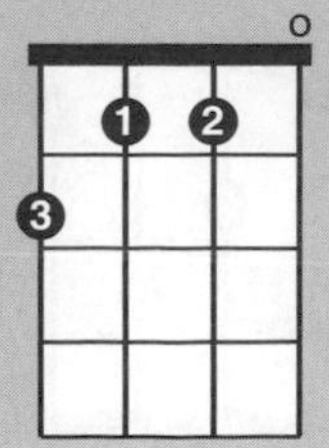

Diminished
D♭°

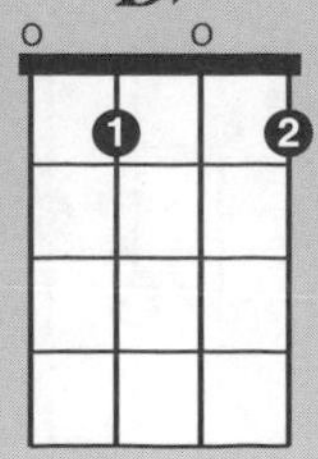

Dominant Ninth
D♭9

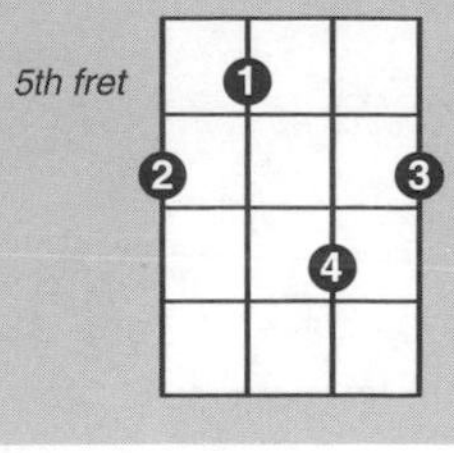

5th fret

Dominant Thirteenth
D♭13

4th fret

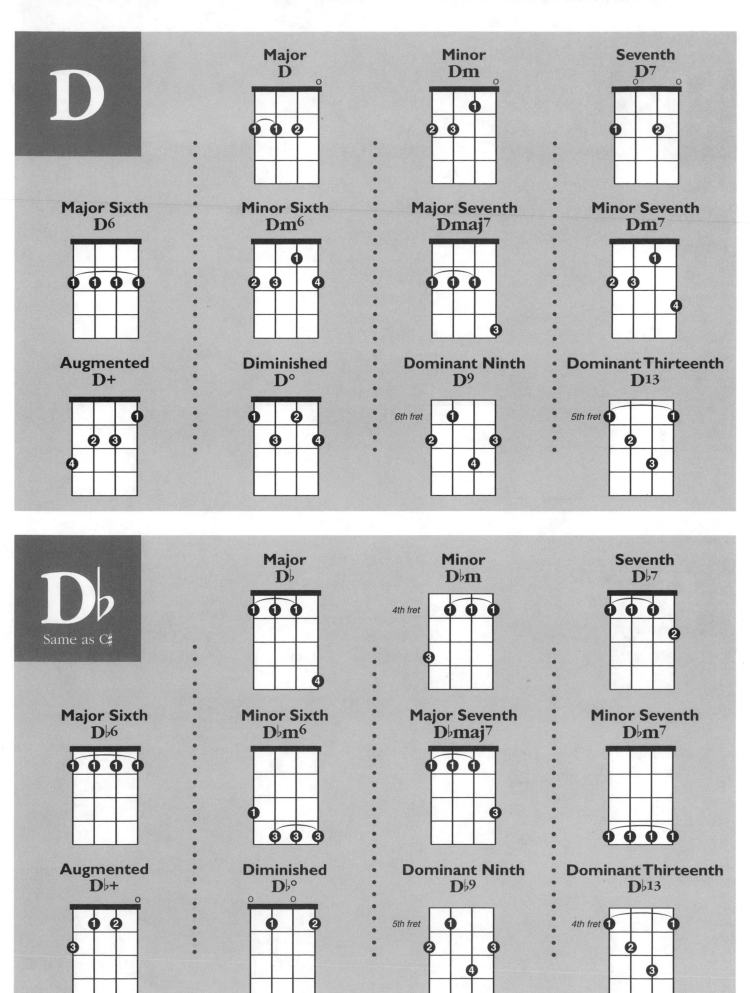

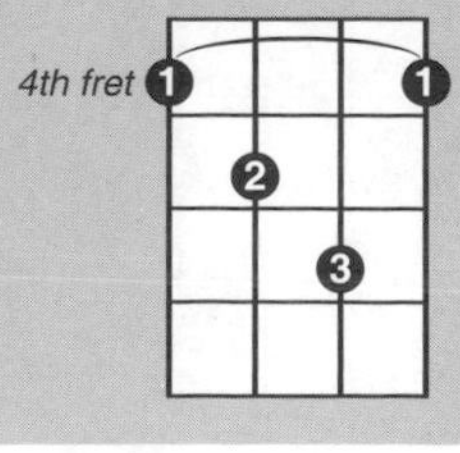

E

Major
E

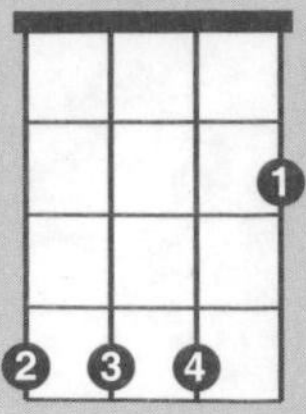

Minor
Em

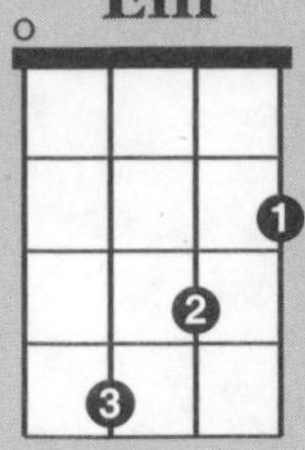

Seventh
E7

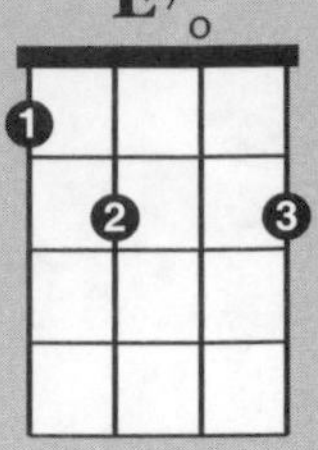

Major Sixth
E6

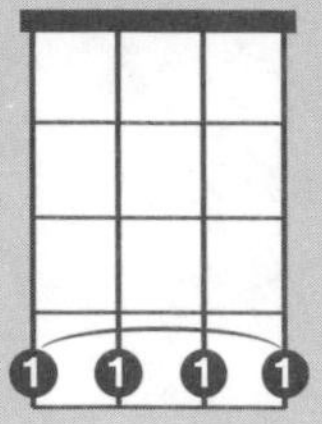

Minor Sixth
Em6

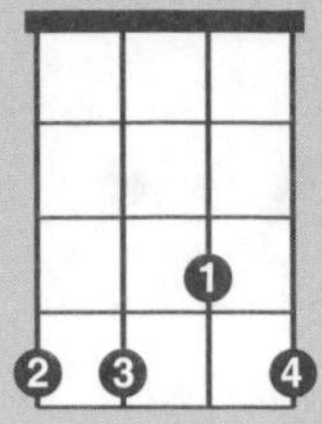

Major Seventh
Emaj7

4th fret

Minor Seventh
Em7

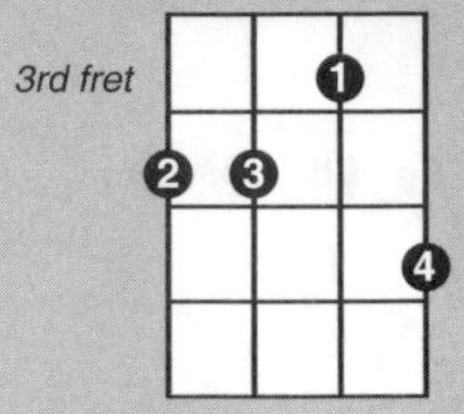

3rd fret

Augmented
E+

Diminished
E°

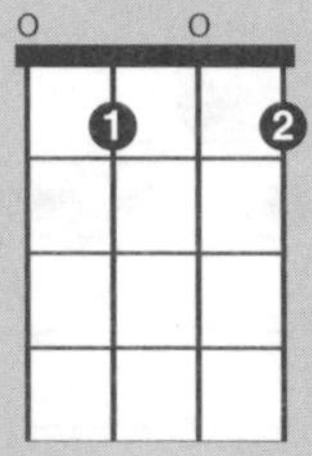

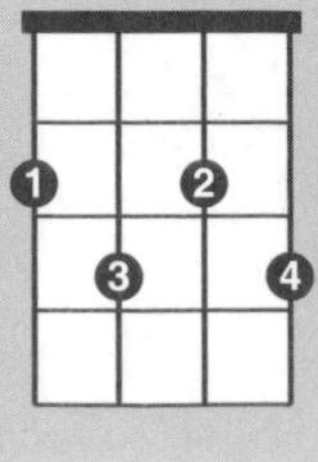

Dominant Ninth
E9

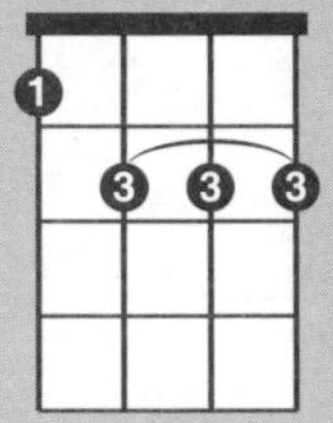

Dominant Thirteenth
E13

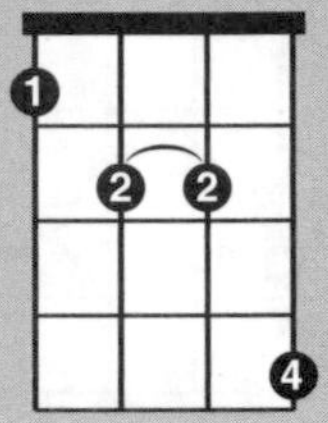

E♭

Same as D♯

Major
E♭

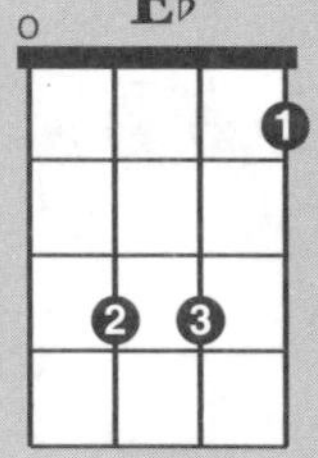

Minor
E♭m

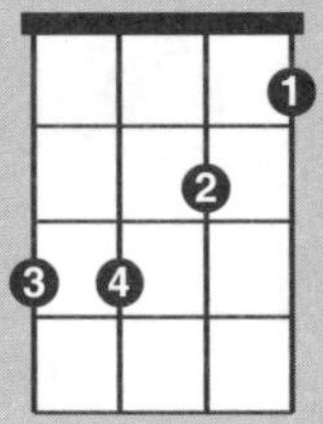

Seventh
E♭7

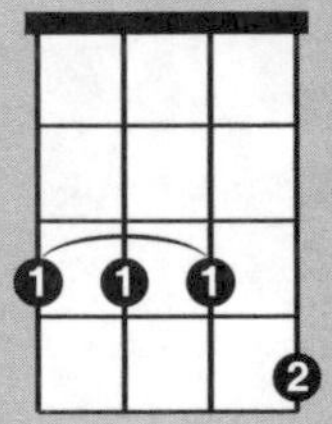

Major Sixth
E♭6

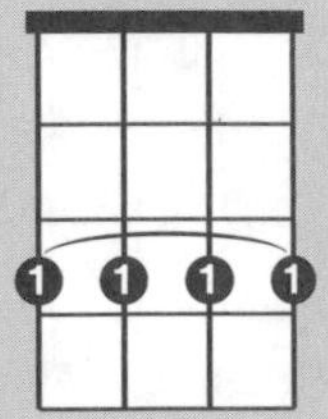

Minor Sixth
E♭m6

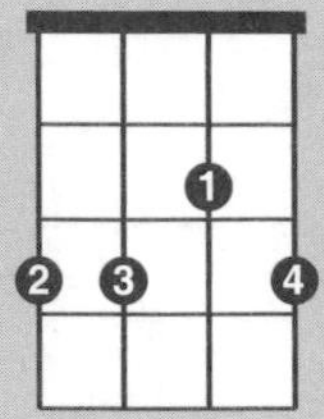

Major Seventh
E♭maj7

3rd fret

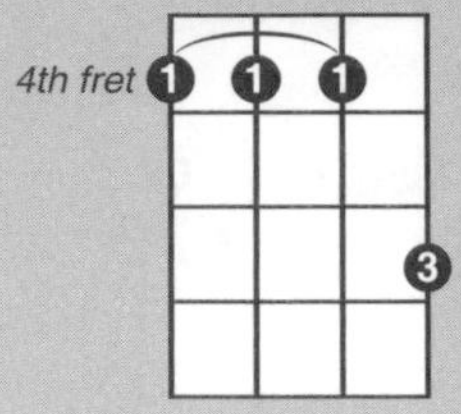

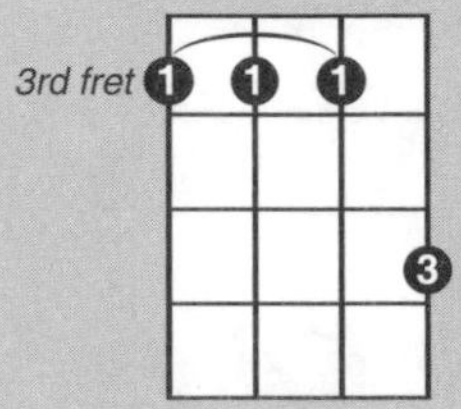

Minor Seventh
E♭m7

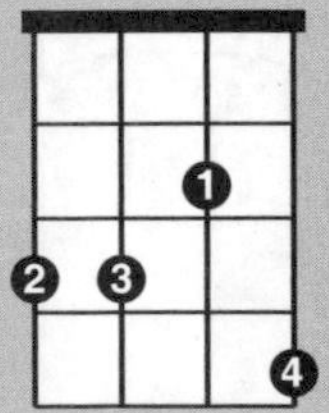

Augmented
E♭+

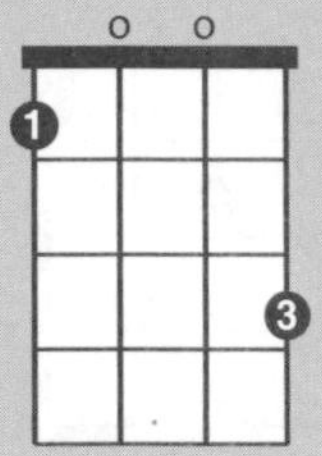

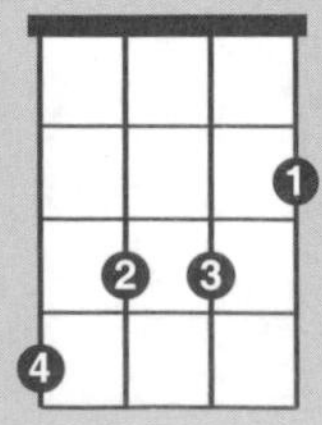

Diminished
E♭°

Dominant Ninth
E♭9

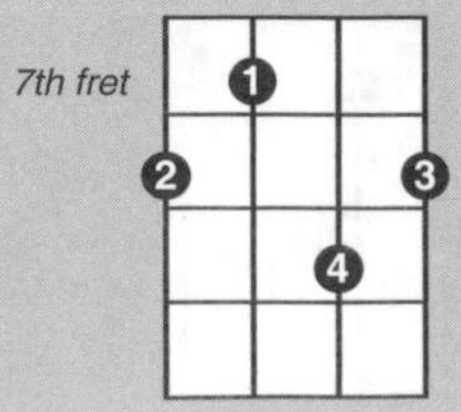

7th fret

Dominant Thirteenth
E♭13

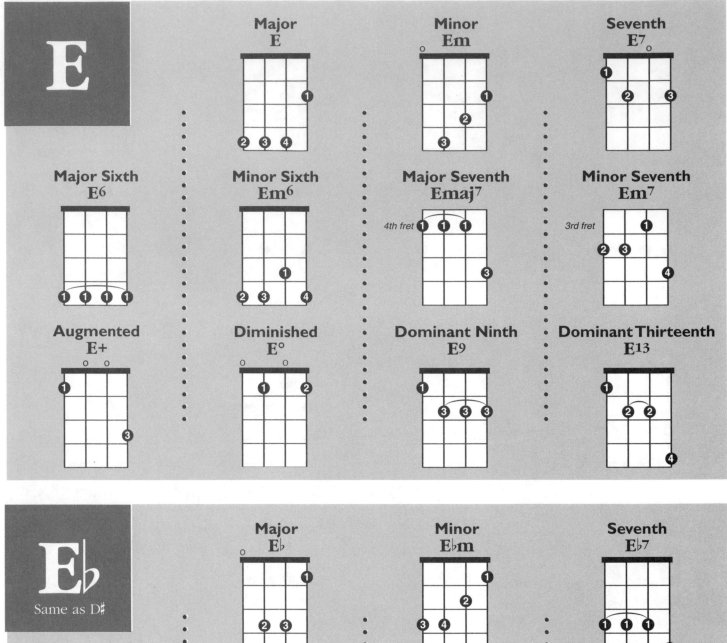

6th fret

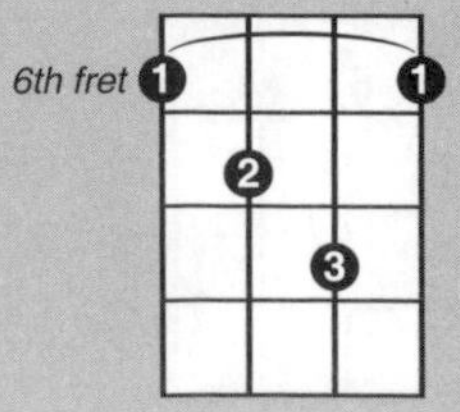

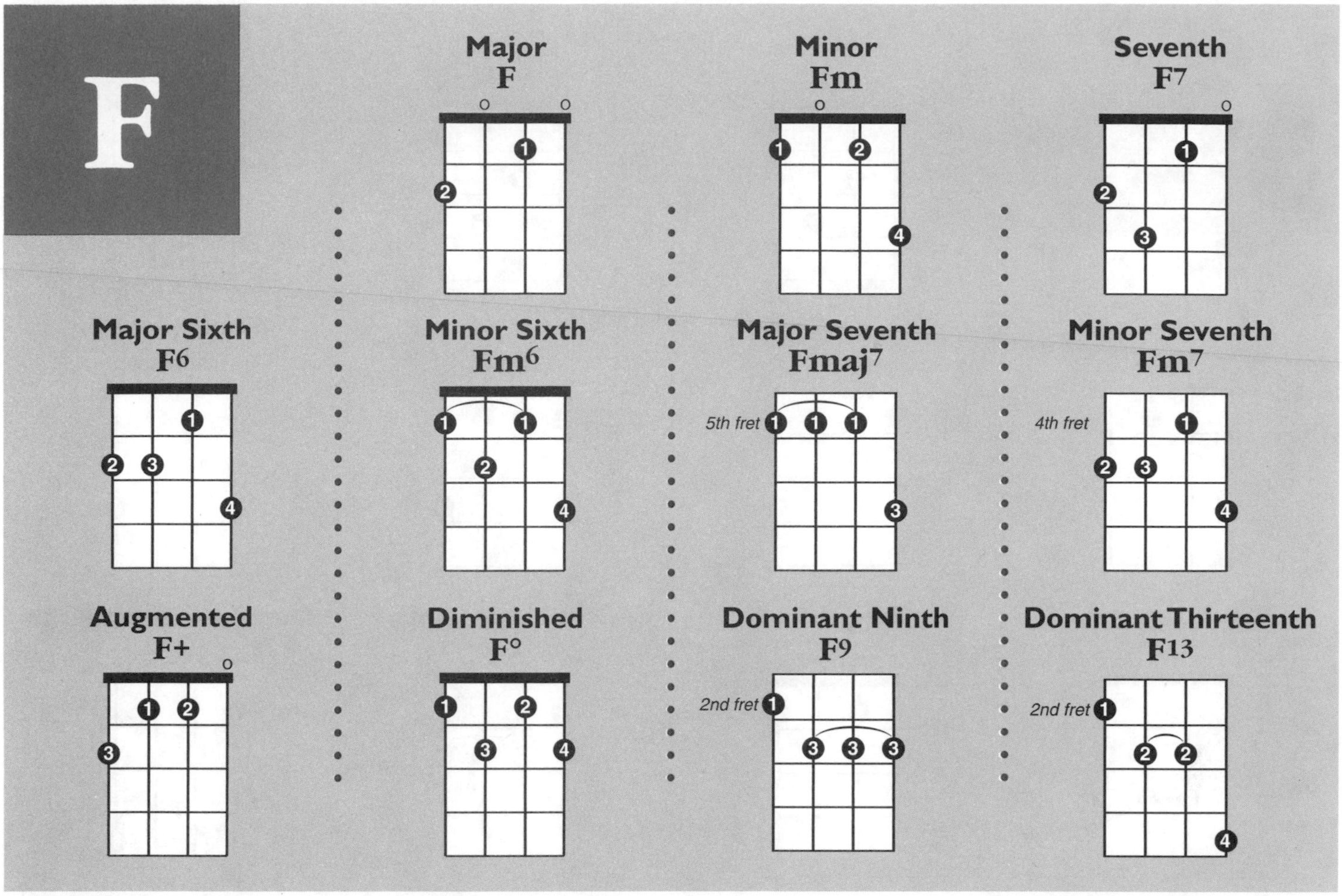

F

Major
F

Minor
Fm

Seventh
F^7

Major Sixth
F^6

Minor Sixth
Fm^6

Major Seventh
$Fmaj^7$

5th fret

Minor Seventh
Fm^7

4th fret

Augmented
F+

Diminished
F°

Dominant Ninth
F^9

2nd fret

Dominant Thirteenth
F^{13}

2nd fret

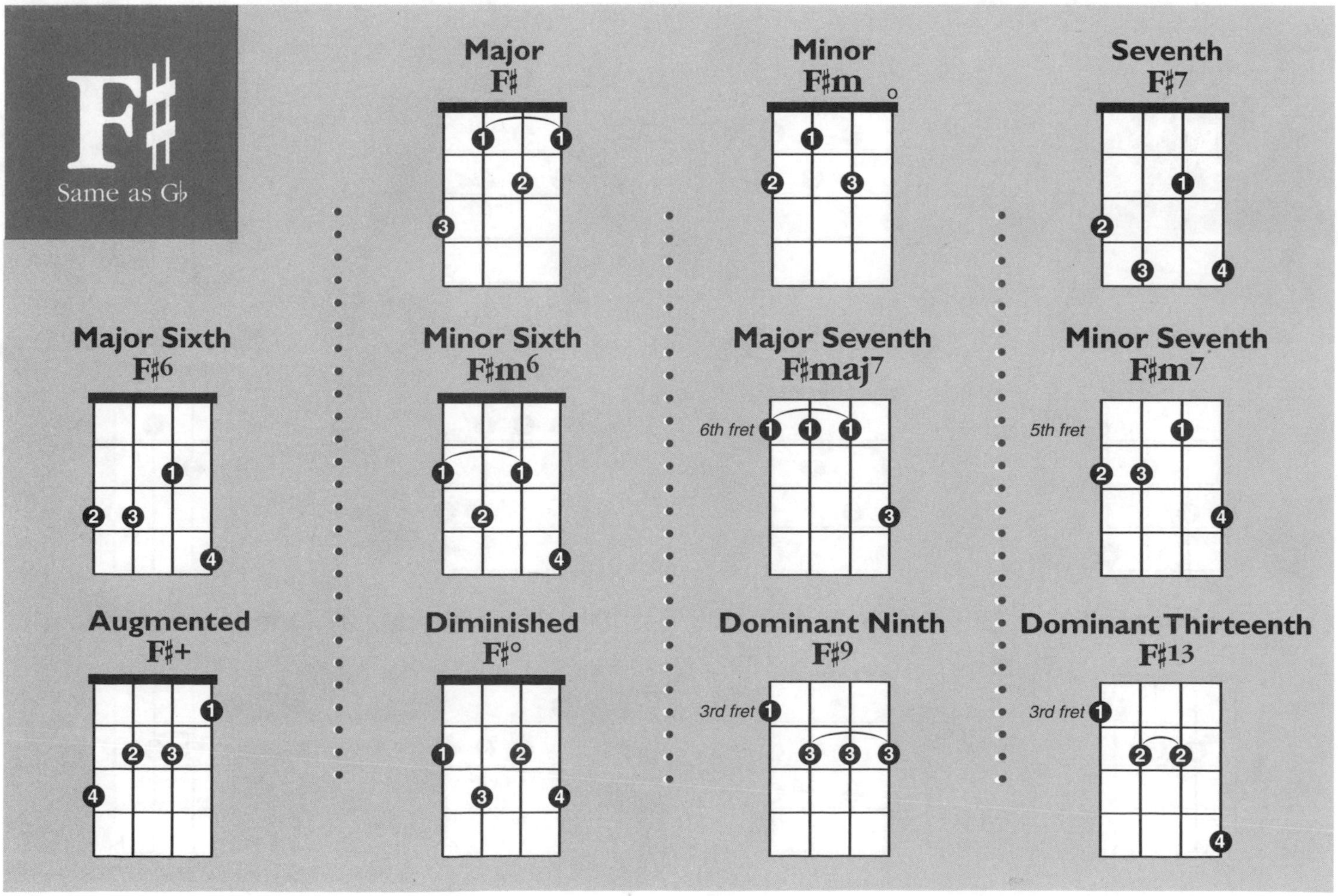

F♯

Same as G♭

Major
F♯

Minor
F♯m

Seventh
$F♯^7$

Major Sixth
$F♯^6$

Minor Sixth
$F♯m^6$

Major Seventh
$F♯maj^7$

6th fret

Minor Seventh
$F♯m^7$

5th fret

Augmented
F♯+

Diminished
F♯°

Dominant Ninth
$F♯^9$

3rd fret

Dominant Thirteenth
$F♯^{13}$

3rd fret

G

Major
G

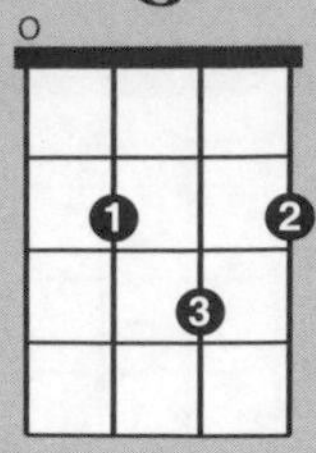

Minor
Gm

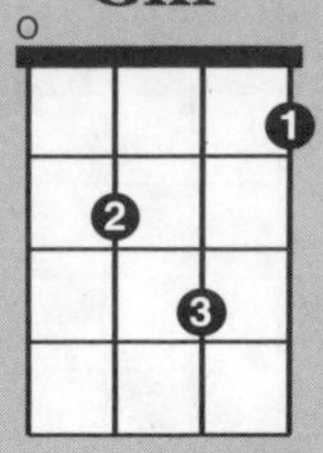

Seventh
G7

Major Sixth
G6
3rd fret

Minor Sixth
Gm6
3rd fret

Major Seventh
Gmaj7
7th fret

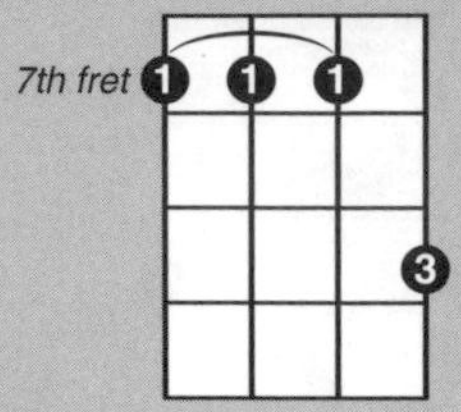

Minor Seventh
Gm7
6th fret

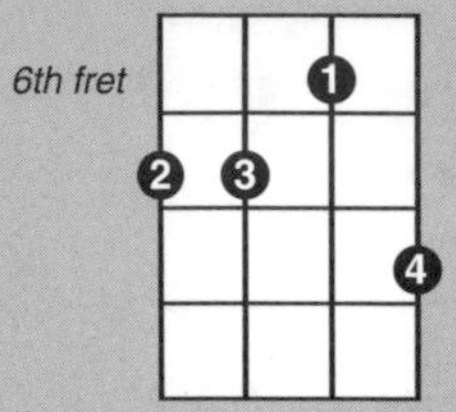

Augmented
G+

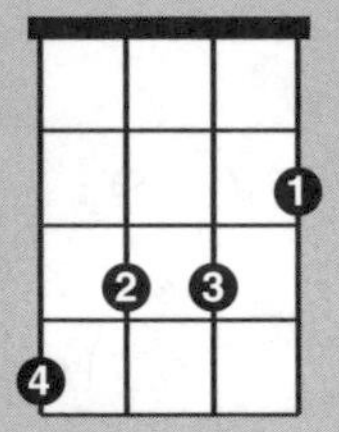

Diminished
G°

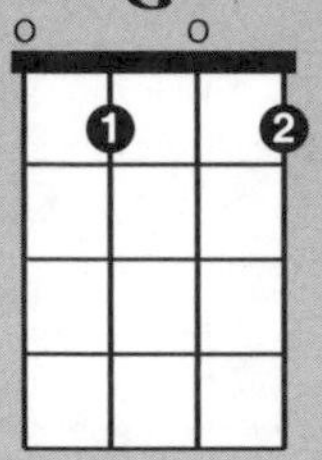

Dominant Ninth
G9
4th fret

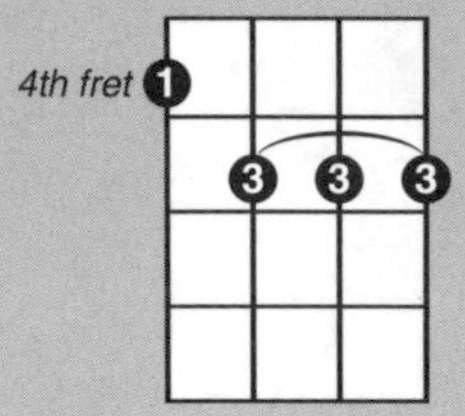

Dominant Thirteenth
G13
4th fret

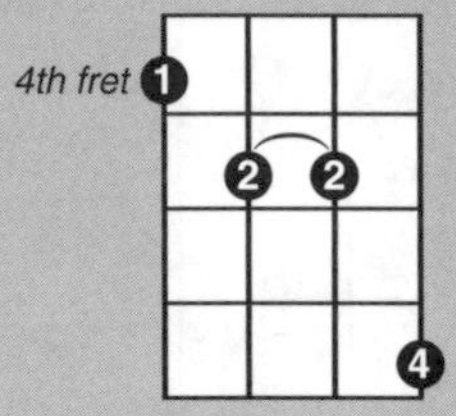

G♭

Same as F♯

Major
G♭

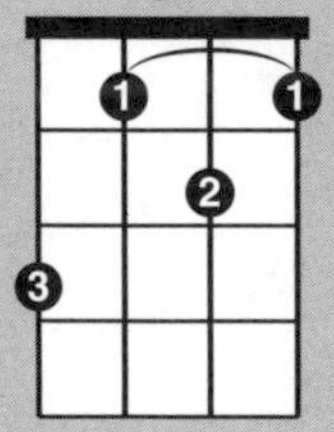

Minor
G♭m

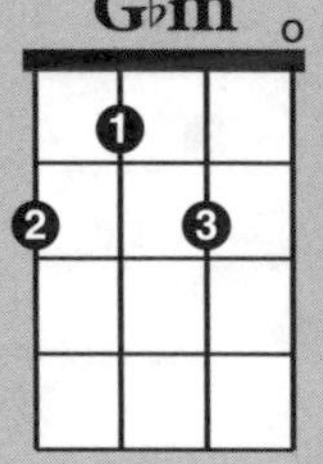

Seventh
G♭7

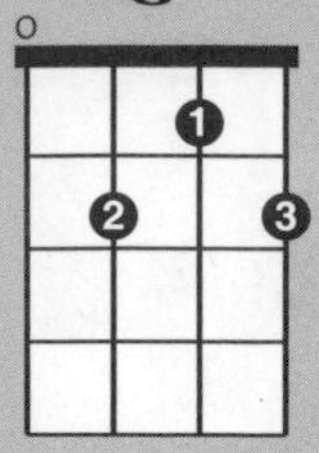

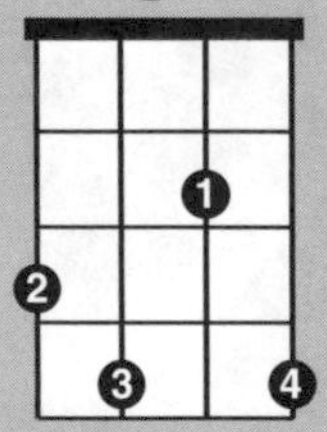

Major Sixth
G♭6

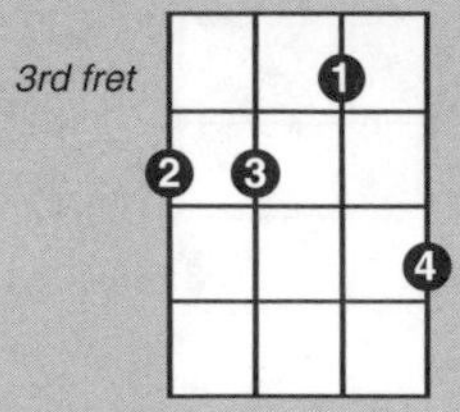

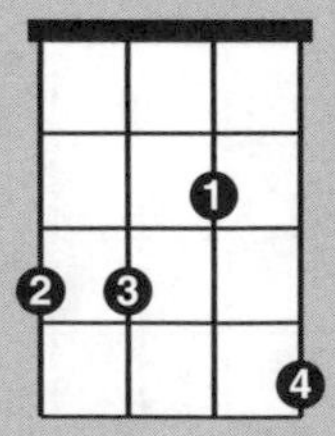

Minor Sixth
G♭m6

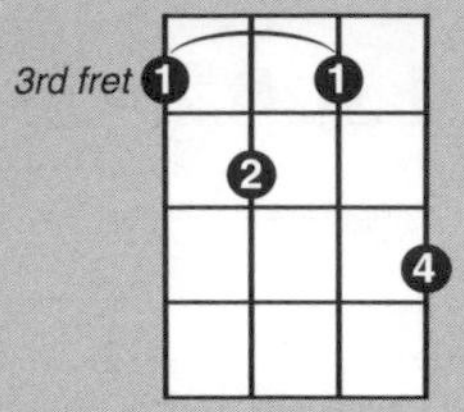

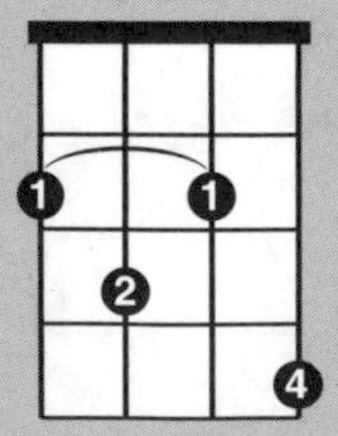

Major Seventh
G♭maj7
6th fret

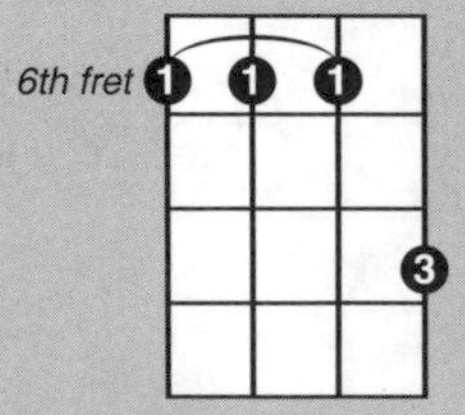

Minor Seventh
G♭m7
5th fret

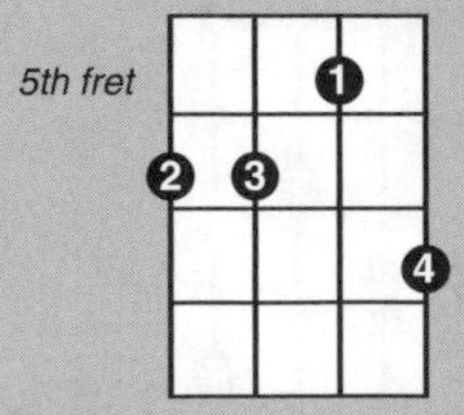

Augmented
G♭+

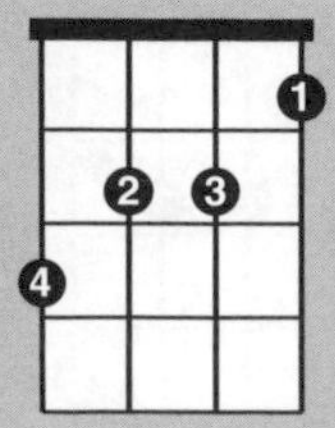

Diminished
G♭°

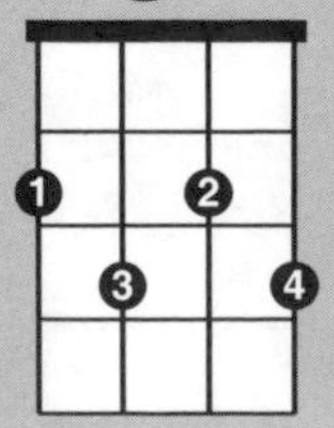

Dominant Ninth
G♭9
3rd fret

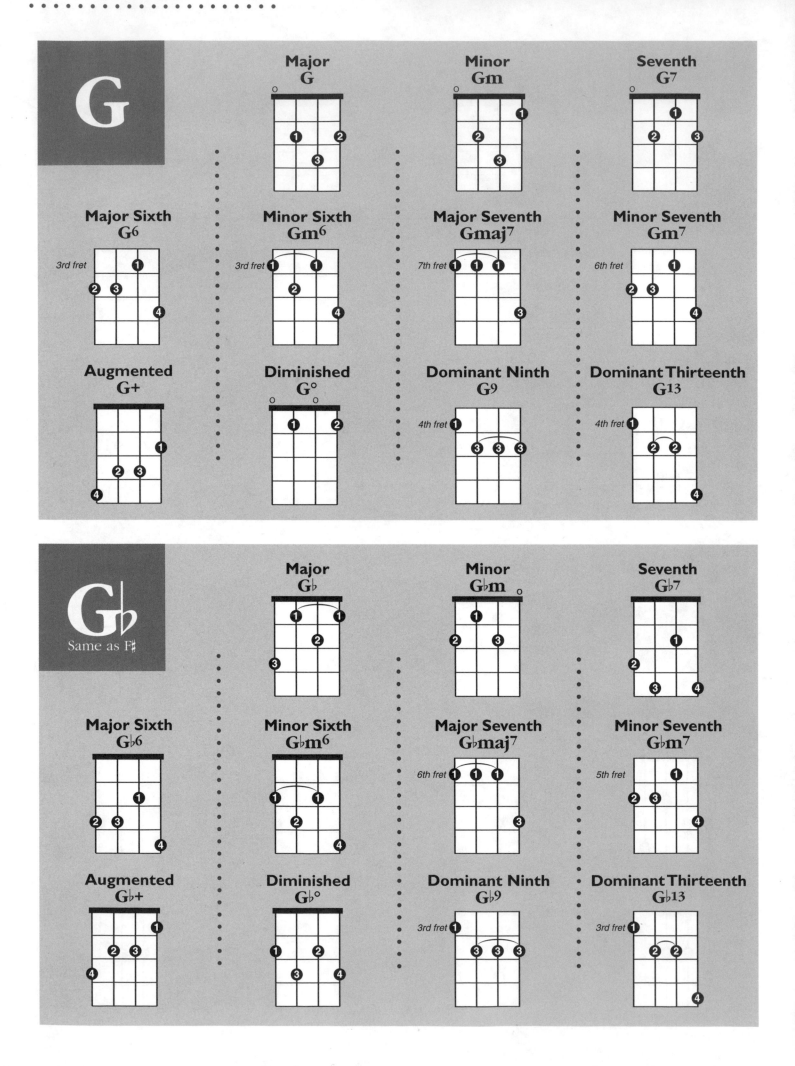

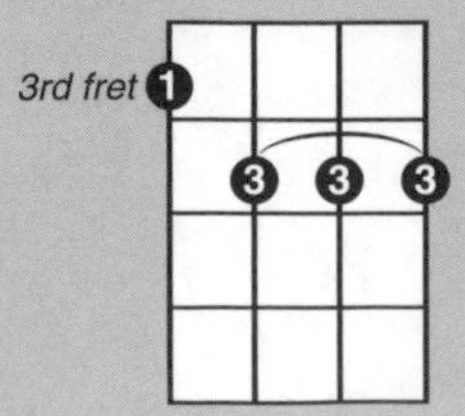

Dominant Thirteenth
G♭13
3rd fret

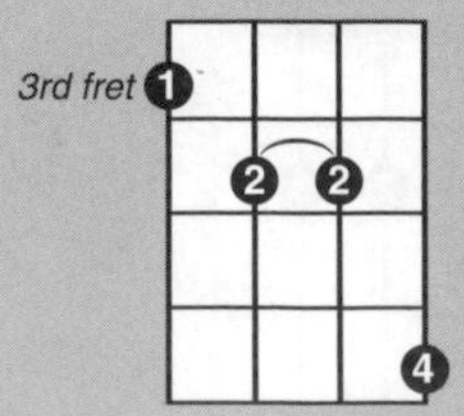